Catechism

A Short Guide to
Orthodox Christianity

For those preparing for Holy Baptism

&

for all those who want to know their faith better

The publication of this book was made possible through

a generous donation from Tom Galioto:

"In memory of my mother, Justine W. Galioto—

for bringing me into the Orthodox Faith and

introducing me to St Vladimir's Seminary."

Metropolitan Hilarion
Alfeyev

Catechism

A Short Guide to Orthodox Christianity

ST VLADIMIR'S SEMINARY PRESS
YONKERS, NEW YORK
2024

Publisher's Cataloging-in-Publication
(Provided by Cassidy Cataloguing Services, Inc.)

Names: Ilarion, Metropolitan of Volokolamsk, 1966- author.

Title: Catechism : a short guide to Orthodox Christianity / Metropolitan Hilarion Alfeyev.

Other titles: Katekhizis. English

Description: Yonkers, New York : St Vladimir's Seminary Press, 2024. | First published in Russian: Katekhizis (Izdatel'skii dom Poznanie, Moskva, 2017). | Includes bibliographical references.

Identifiers: ISBN: 978-0-88141-706-7 (paperback) | 978-0-88141-758-6 (electronic) | LCCN: 2024933629

Subjects: LCSH: Russkai͡a pravoslavnai͡a t͡serkov′--Catechism. | Russkai͡a pravoslavnai͡a t͡serkov′--Doctrines. | Russkai͡a pravoslavnai͡a t͡serkov′--Sacraments. | Orthodox Eastern Church--Catechisms. | Orthodox Eastern Church--Doctrines. | Orthodox Eastern Church--Sacraments.| Religious ethics--Orthodox Eastern Church. | Christianity--Essence, genius, nature. | Faith. | Christian life. | BISAC: RELIGION / Christianity / Orthodox. | RELIGION / Christianity / Catechisms. | RELIGION / Christian Rituals & Practice / Sacraments. | RELIGION / Christian Living / General.

Classification: LCC: BX320.3 .I42213 2024 | DDC: 230/.19--dc23

575 Scarsdale Road, Yonkers, NY 10707
1–800–204–2665 www.svspress.com

ISBN 978-0-88141-706-7 (paper)
ISBN 978-0-88141-758-6 (electronic)

PRINTED IN THE UNITED STATES OF AMERICA

Psalms are quoted from *The Holy Psalter: An Orthodox Christian Translation* (South Canaan, PA / Yonkers, NY: St Tikhon's Monastery Press / St Vladimir's Seminary Press, 2024). Psalms are cited according to the Septuagint (LXX) numbering, which differs from the Hebrew numbering (used by most English translations), thus:

Numbering of the Psalms

Septuagint	Hebrew
1–8	1–8
9	9–10
10–112	11–113
113	114–115
114	116.1–9
115	116.10–19
116–145	117–146
146	147.1–11
147	147.12–20
148–150	148–150

Contents

Abbreviations

ANF The Ante-Nicene Fathers. Edited by Alexander Roberts and James Donaldson. Buffalo, 1885–1887. 10 vols. Repr., Peabody, MA: Hendrickson, 1994.

NPNF[1] The Nicene and Post-Nicene Fathers, Series 1. Edited by Philip Schaff. New York, 1886–1889. 14 vols. Repr., Peabody, MA: Hendrickson, 1994.

NPNF[2] The Nicene and Post-Nicene Fathers, Series 2. Edited by Philip Schaff and Henry Wace. New York, 1890. 14 vols. Repr., Peabody, MA: Hendrickson, 1994.

PPS Popular Patristics Series. Crestwood, NY [Yonkers, NY]: St Vladimir's Seminary Press, 1996–

On notes: Citations to Scripture appear in line, comments or explanations appear in footnotes with Arabic numbers, and source citations appear in endnotes after each section, with Roman numerals.

Foreword

Have you decided to be baptized?

Have you decided to baptize your child?

Were you baptized in infancy, but not brought up in the faith?

Do you visit a church to light a candle, but do not understand the services?

Do you belong to the Orthodox Church, but do not know her teachings?

Have you tried to read the Bible, but cannot understand its meaning?

Do you go to church, but never go to Confession?

Do you go to church, make a Confession, and receive Communion, but do not understand many things and want to deepen your knowledge?

If the answer is "yes" to any of these questions, then this book is for you.

The word "catechism" is of Greek origin. It literally means "oral instruction." A catechism is usually a book in which the basic truths of the Christian faith are set out in short and accessible form. A catechism is a guide to the faith. Its purpose is not to prove, but to expound and explain. The author of the best-known Russian Orthodox catechism is St Philaret of Moscow, a renowned ecclesiastical figure and theologian, and metropolitan of Moscow from 1821 to 1867. To this day his catechism[i] retains its importance as an authoritative exposition of the fundamentals of Orthodox doctrine, approved by the church hierarchy.

Still, almost two hundred years have passed since that book was published. Over this time peoples' way of thinking has changed. Some of the topics have lost their relevance, while at the same time many new questions have arisen to which people seek clear answers.

It is therefore quite natural that new catechisms appear that are both long and short, written either by a group of authors or by individuals.

The catechism that you are holding is an attempt to explain the Orthodox faith and to set out in short form its fundamentals for contemporary readers. It consists of three parts.

The first part explains the basic doctrinal truths of the Orthodox Church concerning the faith, God, Jesus Christ, the Holy Spirit, the Church, Baptism, and the resurrection of the dead.

The second part is devoted to moral topics. In it, we talk about the Ten Commandments of the Old Testament, the Beatitudes from the Sermon on the Mount, love of God and love of neighbor, sin and repentance, the various issues of family ethics, the upbringing of children, and the place of women in the Church.

In the third part we speak about prayer and worship, the church building and icons, the church calendar and church holidays, the Divine Liturgy and other church services, and the sacraments and rites of the Church.

And so, let us begin our journey.

We will tread this path together, you and I—the author of this book and a bishop of the Russian Orthodox Church.

And may the Lord Jesus Christ Himself accompany us on this path.

---

[i] Philaret of Moscow, *The Longer Catechism of the Orthodox, Catholic, Eastern Church*, trans. R. W. Blackmore (Aberdeen, 1845); reprinted in Philip Schaff, *Creeds of Christendom, with a History and Critical Notes:* Vol. 2: *The Greek and Latin Creeds, with Translations* (New York: Harper & Brothers, 1919), 445–542. [Hereafter Philaret, *Catechism*, followed by the question number and then the page number. Note that the work can be found online on various websites, and at least one hardcopy reprint is available.]

I

Doctrine

The Faith

The One God—Father and Creator

Jesus Christ

The Holy Spirit

The Trinity

The Church

Baptism

The Resurrection of the Dead

Christ and apostles. Duccio di Buoninsegna. Italy. 14th c.

The Christian faith is an integrated system based on the teaching of Jesus Christ. The Church has interpreted and set out this teaching in the language of theological definitions or **dogmas**—that is, doctrinal truths. Believing them is the fundamental condition of membership of the Church.

We will master the basics of Christian teaching by following step by step the text of the Creed—a short exposition of the basic Christian dogmas that received its definitive shape in the fourth century.

I believe in one God,
the Father Almighty,
Maker of heaven and earth and
of all things visible and invisible;

and in one Lord Jesus Christ,
the Son of God, the Only-begotten,
begotten of the Father before all ages:
Light of light; true God of true God;
begotten, not made;
of one essence with the Father;
by whom all things were made;

who for us men and for our salvation
came down from heaven, and was
incarnate of the Holy Spirit and the
Virgin Mary, and became man;

and He was crucified for us
under Pontius Pilate, and suffered,
and was buried;

and the third day He arose again,
according to the Scriptures, and
ascended into heaven,
and sits at the right hand of the Father;
and He shall come again with glory to
judge the living and the dead;
whose kingdom shall have no end;

and in the Holy Spirit, the Lord,
the Giver of life,
who proceeds from the Father;
who with the Father and the Son
together is worshipped and glorified;
who spoke by the prophets;

in one Holy, Catholic, and
Apostolic Church.
I acknowledge one Baptism for the
remission of sins.
I look for the resurrection of the dead
and the life of the world to come.

Amen.

1. The Faith

The Creed begins with the words "I believe." This points towards faith as the foundation of the relationship between the human person and God.

What Is Faith?

Many people call themselves Christians. Some of them, though, do not know the basics of their own religion and cannot even distinguish it from other religions. Some say: "I don't go to church, but I have God in my heart." To the question of how one perceives God, one often hears varied answers such as: "I believe in something radiant and good"; "I believe in goodness. After all, the most important thing is to be good, while there is no obligation to visit a church and observe the rituals."

Why is it not enough to "have God in one's heart"? Why is it not enough to believe in some abstract and remote principle of good? Because faith is not simply an intellectual or rational conviction in the existence of God, or of another world, or of higher powers. **Faith is a way of life** founded upon communion with God. Faith presupposes a personal encounter of the human being with God.

The path to faith is mysterious and, in many ways, impossible to explain. There is, however, in the Christian tradition the notion that religious feeling is natural to the soul of all human beings. The Latin author Tertullian (second to third centuries) called the soul "Christian by its nature."[i] Another western author, St Augustine (fourth century), addresses to God the following words: "You created us for yourself, and our heart is restless until it rests in You."[ii] We may say that every person has an inner predisposition towards faith, an innate striving towards his Maker. Nonetheless, this natural religious feeling is not manifested in every person.

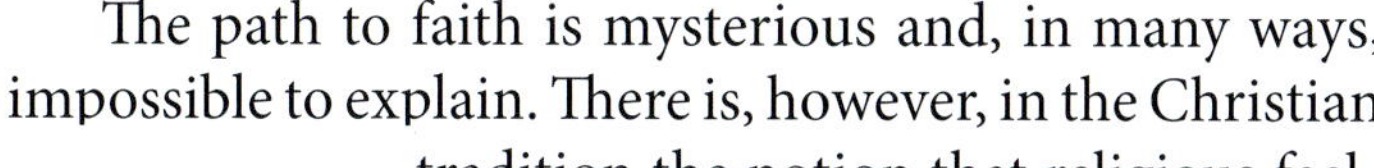

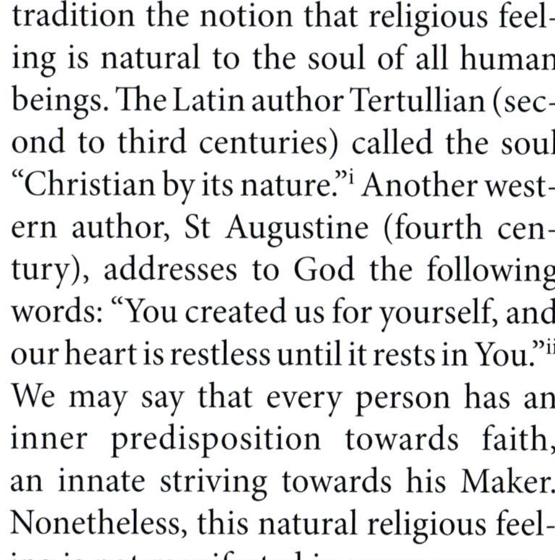

Prophet Isaiah's Prayer. Illuminated manuscript. Byzantium. 15th c.

Faith is a fire that is ignited in the heart of the human person. Over many centuries the fire of faith has inspired people to great deeds and heroic accomplishments. Faith has inspired people who have stood for their beliefs and were ready to surrender their lives for them. Faith was the spiritual power that helped the martyrs to endure the cruelest torments, helped those that were led to their execution to live through their last moments on earth and greet their hour of death. And this happened not only in the first few centuries, but also in quite recent times when enormous efforts and means were employed to expunge faith from people's hearts, and when the bearers of faith—the priests, monks, and laity—were physically exterminated.

Faith is the inner zeal and readiness to dedicate all one's creative powers, all one's life, to the service of a higher ideal. Faith has helped artists, architects, musicians, poets, and writers to create magnificent works of art. For many centuries the Christian faith has fertilized the cultural life of humanity, and a multitude of outstanding works of art have been inspired by the ideals of faith.

Faith as Obedience to God

The Epistle to the Hebrews gives us the following definition: "Now faith is the substance of things hoped for, the evidence of things not seen. ... By faith we understand that the worlds were framed by the word of God, so that the things which are seen were not made of things

Sacrifice of Isaac. Mosaic. Ravenna, Italy. 6th c.

which are visible" (Heb 11.1, 3). The text presents us with the example of the biblical patriarch Abraham: "By faith Abraham obeyed when he was called to set out for a place that he was to receive as an inheritance; and he set out, not knowing where he was going. By faith he stayed for a time in the land he had been promised ... For he looked forward to the city that has foundations, whose architect and builder is God ... By faith Abraham, when put to the test, offered up Isaac ... He considered the fact that God is able even to raise someone from the dead" (Heb 11.8–10, 17, 19).

The Bible (Gen 22.2–12) narrates how God promised the hundred-year-old Abraham and his barren wife Sarah a child, how the old couple waited many years for the fulfillment of this promise, how their long-awaited son was born and then how, when the boy grew up, God tested Abraham by saying: "Take now your son, your only son Isaac, whom you love, and go to the land of Moriah, and offer him there as a burnt offering on one of the mountains of which I shall tell you." Abraham obeys this command and sets off on a journey with his son and servants.

On the third day he sees from afar the place indicated by God and says to his servants: "Stay here with the donkey; the lad and I will go yonder and worship, and we will come back to you." When Isaac sees that Abraham did not take the sacrificial animal with him, he asks his father: "Look, the fire and the wood, but where is the lamb for a burnt offering?" Abraham replies: "My son, God will provide for Himself the lamb for a burnt offering."

Finally, father and son come to the place indicated by God, Abraham binds Isaac, lays him on the altar and takes a knife in order to slay him. At that moment he hears the voice of an angel: "Do not lay your hand on the lad, or do anything to him; for now I know that you fear God, since you have not withheld your son, your only son, from Me."

Abraham is justly called the "father of all those who believe" (Rom 4.11). A significant part of the first book of the Bible (Gen 11.26–25.9) is taken up with a description of his life where he is presented as an exemplar of absolute and undivided devotion to God. He demonstrated with his life what faith is and how it should be. **To believe is to trust, to love, to be obedient.** The Christian trusts God more than himself, loves God more than himself, and strives to fulfill God's commandments more than his own will.

From the Dead Sea Scrolls. A comment to the Book of the Prophet Habakkuk. c. 1st c. BC–1st c.

Divine Revelation

The Christian faith is not the fruit of human creativity or human wisdom. It is founded upon **divine revelation**—that is, on the notion that God desired to reveal Himself to people in order that, for their salvation, they might believe in Him correctly and worship Him rightly.[iii]

The substance of divine revelation is expressed in the Epistle to the Hebrews in the following words: "God, who at various times and in various ways spoke in time past to the fathers by the prophets, has in these last days spoken to us by His Son, whom He has appointed heir of all things, through whom also He made the worlds" (Heb 1.1–2). This indicates that God revealed Himself to people gradually and in stages: the first stage was God's revelation through the prophets, while the second was through His Son Jesus Christ.

Scripture and Holy Tradition

The two stages of divine revelation are mirrored in the **Christian Scripture**—the Bible.[1] It is divided into two parts—the Old Testament and the New Testament.

The Old Testament is a collection of books devoted to the history of humanity from the creation of the world and the history of the chosen people of Israel. An important place in this collection is occupied by the books of the prophets, who foretold the Savior's coming into the world.

The New Testament contains the four books of the Gospels, which narrate the life, sufferings, death, and Resurrection of Jesus Christ, the book of the Acts of the Apostles devoted to the beginnings of the life of the Christian Church, the Catholic[2] epistles of the apostles devoted to various aspects of the Christian faith and morality; the Epistles of the Apostle Paul, which open up a broad spectrum of theological and moral themes; and Revelation (also called the Apocalypse)—a book of prophetic visions devoted to the end of the history of the world and the second coming of Christ.

[1] "Bible" comes from the Greek word *biblia*, meaning "books."

[2] The word "Catholic" has different meanings. In this instance it means that these epistles are not addressed to one individual church community (Romans, Corinthians, and so on). Sometimes these are called the "general" epistles.

The Church calls all the books of Scripture "divinely inspired," for, although their authors were human, they wrote under the guidance of the Holy Spirit,[3] at His inspiration.

Scripture is the authoritative and indisputable source of faith for Christians. It is a part of Holy Tradition and it is only from within Tradition that it is possible to interpret it correctly.

By **Holy Tradition** in the Orthodox Church we mean the teaching, sacraments, rites, moral precepts, and the multi-faceted diversity of the spiritual experience communicated to the faithful from generation to generation in both written and oral form.

2. The One God—Father and Creator

The Creed begins with the words: "I believe in one God, the Father Almighty, Maker of heaven and earth and of all things visible and invisible."

God Is One

Here the fundamental dogma of the Christian faith is affirmed above all—that **there is only one God**.

Christianity is a monotheistic religion.[4] Christianity inherited the belief in the one God from the religion of the ancient Hebrews as reflected in the Old Testament.

The God of whom the Old Testament speaks is the one and only God: "Before Me there was no God formed, nor shall there be after Me. I, even I, am the Lord, and besides

[3] More will be said about the Holy Spirit on pages 68–72.

[4] **Monotheism** (from the Greek *monos*, meaning "one," and *theos*, meaning "god") is the belief in one God. The other monotheistic religions are Judaism and Islam. Sometimes Christianity, Judaism, and Islam are called the "Abrahamic religions" from the biblical Abraham, who is venerated in all three religious traditions.

Me there is no savior" (Is 43.10–11). The first commandment of the law of Moses states: "I am the Lord your God ... You shall have no other gods before Me" (Ex 20.2–3). In the Book of Deuteronomy God speaks of Himself: "Hear, O Israel: The Lord our God, the Lord is one! You shall love the Lord your God with all your heart, with all your soul, and with all your strength" (Deut 6.4–5).

Jesus Christ repeatedly pointed towards the importance of the Old Testament commandment to worship only the one God. He replied to the tempter: "You shall worship the Lord your God, and Him only you shall serve" (Mt 4.10; Lk 4.8). Jesus replied to the scribe who asked, "Which is the first commandment of all?" thus: "The first of all the commandments is: 'Hear, O Israel, the Lord our God, the Lord is one. And you shall love the Lord your God with all your heart, with all your soul, with all your mind, and with all your strength'" (Mk 12. 28–30).

The Apostle Paul states: "There is no other God but one. For even if there are so-called gods, whether in heaven or on earth ... yet for us there is one God, the Father,[5] of whom are all things, and we for Him; and one Lord Jesus Christ, through whom are all things, and through whom we live" (1 Cor 8.4–6).

The Idea of God in the Old Testament

The God of the Old Testament is by no means an abstract power remote from people. He is the "**living God**" (1 Kgs 17.26; 2 Sam 19.16), He is always alive and active,

[5] The meaning of these words is that though various fantastical beings in heaven and objects deified by people on earth may be called gods, in truth there is only one God. Here the apostle is referring to the various forms of **polytheism** (from the Greek *polloi*, meaning "many," and *theos*, meaning "god"), or paganism. Among the polytheistic religions were, in particular, the religions of ancient Greece and Rome. There have survived into our times polytheistic religions such as Hinduism, Taoism, Jainism, Shintoism, and others.

Archangel Michael and three youths in the Babylonian furnace. Illuminated manuscript. Byzantium. 14th c.

He shall neither "slumber nor sleep" (Ps 120.4), He "neither faints nor is weary" (Is 40.28).

God in the Old Testament is "**holy**" (Is 57.15), His name is "holy and terrible" (Ps 110.9). He is called "good" (Ps 33.8; 99.5; 144.9). He is absolute good, the source of all good and all holiness. God is the "**Judge** of all the earth" (Gen 18.25); He will "plead His case with all flesh. He will give those who are wicked to the sword" (Jer 25.31). He is the righteous Judge, who ascends the throne and judges rightly (Ps 9.7–8); He "puts down one and lifts up another" (Ps 74.7); He gives to the proud their just deserts (Ps 93.2).

Many Old Testament texts mention God in a metaphorical sense as a human-like being having a face, eyes, ears, hands, feet, breath; they state that God sees, hears, speaks, walks, turns over and turns away, remembers and forgets, is angry and soothed, is surprised, grieves, hates, and repents.

At the basis of this metaphorical language lies the experience of a personal encounter with God, the sense of His constant participation in the life of people. The ancients felt God to be alongside them—He was their king and ruler, was present at their worship and festivals, helped them in their everyday lives. They expressed their experience of communicating with Him using the accessible means of human images and concepts.

The Idea of God in the New Testament

In the New Testament God is revealed through Jesus Christ primarily as the **heavenly Father**. In the Old Testament the name "Father" was sometimes used for

God (Is 63.16), but in the sense that He is the father of the people of Israel. In the New Testament, however, the notion that God is the father of all people is insistently and consistently presented.[6]

God has a plan for every human being, and every person in God's eyes is precious. For God there are no superfluous people, there is no one who would not be worthy of His attention and love. God remembers every one of His creatures: "Are not two sparrows sold for a copper coin? And not one of them falls to the ground apart from your Father's will. But the very hairs of your head are all numbered. Do not fear therefore; you are of more value than many sparrows" (Mt 10.29–31).

Jesus says of His heavenly Father that He is "merciful" (Lk 6.36), that He is "kind to the unthankful and evil" (Lk 6.35), that He "makes His sun rise on the evil and on the good, and sends rain on the just and the unjust" (Mt 5.45).

No human kindness is comparable with **God's goodness**. It is in this sense that Jesus says that "No one is good but One, that is, God" (Mt 19.17; Mk 10.18). At the same time, He calls upon His followers to imitate God in His perfection (Mt 5.48), reminding them that mercy likens them to God (Lk 6.36), and that peace-making makes them the children of God (Mt 5.9).

On the foundation of the religion of the Old Testament Jesus created a new religion—a religion that makes people the sons and daughters of God. Adoption in God happens through the guidance of the Holy Spirit: "For as many as are led by the Spirit of God, these are sons of God. For you did not receive the spirit of bondage again to fear, but you received the Spirit of adoption by whom we cry out, 'Abba, Father.' The Spirit Himself bears witness with our spirit that we are children of God" (Rom 8.14–16).

[6] In the teaching of Jesus Christ in the Gospel of Matthew the phrase "heavenly Father" (always with the possessive pronouns "Your" or "My") is encountered in total twenty times.

The Qualities of God

Scripture testifies that **God is incomprehensible**: "Oh, the depth of the riches both of the wisdom and knowledge of God! How unsearchable are His judgments and His ways past finding out! 'For who has known the mind of the Lord? Or who has become His counselor?'" (Rom 11.33–34). In being incomprehensible by His nature, God nonetheless revealed Himself throughout the ages to people through His actions, through the prophets, and through His chosen one, Jesus Christ (Heb 1.1–2; 3.1).

Scripture bears witness that **God is invisible**. In the Old Testament God spoke to Moses: "You cannot see My face; for no man shall see Me, and live" (Ex 33.20). But the New Testament became the revelation of the invisible God through His Son. In the Gospel of John the meaning of this revelation is expressed thus: "No one has seen God at any time. The only begotten Son, who is in the bosom of the Father, He has declared Him" (Jn 1.18).

Jesus Christ says that "**God is Spirit**" (Jn 4.24). This means that God does not have a body, is not material, is not confined by space or time. St Philaret of Moscow writes that "God is a Spirit, eternal, all-good, omniscient, all-just, almighty, omnipresent, unchangeable, all-sufficing to himself, all-blessed."[iv]

The New Testament states that "**God is light** and in him there is no darkness at all" (1 Jn 1.5). The word "light" here is used metaphorically: the light symbolizes the good, while the darkness symbolizes evil. It does not mean the light that can be perceived by physical sight. According to the Apostle Paul, God dwells "in unapproachable light, whom no man has seen or can see" (1 Tim 6.16). St Gregory the Theologian (fourth century) compares God to the sun: "The highest light is God, unapproachable and ineffable, neither grasped by the mind nor expressed in language. It illumines every reason-endowed nature. It is to intelligible realities what the sun is to sense-perceptible realities."[v]

The New Testament testifies that "**God is love**" (1 Jn 4.8, 16). He does not merely possess love directed at something external to Him: He *is* love within Himself, within His very being, while His love is manifested to those outside Him. One such manifestation of Divine Love was the creation of the world and the human person.

God as Maker of the Universe

God created the universe in all its diversity and beauty. The sun, the moon, the planets, the stars, and the galaxies—all of the visible cosmos was created by the one almighty God, the "Maker of heaven and earth, and all things visible and invisible."

God is the Ruler of all, for He not only created the whole universe but also upholds it within His hand—that is, He governs it and cares for it, He sustains its life. The world exists only thanks to its connection with its Maker: the world cannot exist independently of God. The creative word of God that made the world, to use the figurative comparison of St Philaret of Moscow, is a

Creation of fish and birds. Mosaic. Saint Mark's Basilica. Venice, Italy. 13th c.

diamond bridge upon which all that has been created is placed and stands "beneath the Divine abyss of infinity and beyond the abyss of its own worthlessness."[vi]

Not all people believe that the universe was created by God: some propose that it appeared by itself and that no one rules over it. The presence of the **Maker** in the universe is revealed to people through faith thanks to which ever "since the creation of the world His invisible attributes are clearly seen, being understood by the things that are made" (Rom 1.20).

The majesty and diversity of the world testify to the notion that it has a Maker. Like a painting that cannot appear by itself without an artist, the universe could not have appeared without its Creator. Like a watch that could not be made without a watchmaker and would be unable to work if it were not wound up, the universe cannot exist without the One who created it and who governs it.

Why did God create the world? Christian theology answers this question thus: the reason for the

creation of the world was **God's goodness:** "It was not sufficient for the goodness to be moved only in contemplation of itself, but it was necessary that the good be poured forth and spread outward."[vii] God "was not satisfied with contemplating Himself but out of a superabundance of goodness was pleased that things should come into being that would benefit from His goodness and share in it."[viii]

Since He is absolute good, God wanted created beings to exist so that they might partake of this good. In being love, God desired that His love extend also to the whole world that He had created.

The Creation of the World and the Human Person

The Bible narrates the creation of the world and the human person. It opens with the words: "In the beginning God created the heavens and the earth" (Gen 1.1). It further tells of how God created the light and separated it from the darkness, created the heavens, the sea and dry land, the lights under the heavenly firmament, the fish in the sea, all things that crawl, the animals on the earth and the birds in the skies (Gen 1.2–25). Finally, God created "man in His own image; in the image of God He created him; male and female He created them. Then God blessed them, and God said to them, 'Be fruitful and multiply; and fill the earth and subdue it'" (Gen 1.27–28).

Adam names the animals. Mosaic. Saint Mark's Basilica. Venice, Italy. 13th c.

The biblical narrative of the six days of creation should not be understood literally. The psalms state that "a thousand years in Your sight are but as yesterday that is past" (Ps 89.4). And according to the Apostle Peter, "with the Lord one day is as a thousand years, and a thousand years as one day" (2 Pet 3.8). The biblical six days can be understood as the six consecutive stages of creation which unfold gradually, rather like a majestic painting by a great Artist. Each stage, though, could last as long as is necessary—it is by no means obligatory to understand them as calendar days, even more so as the sun was created only on the fourth day.

The biblical teaching on the creation of the human person according to **the image and likeness of God** lies at the basis of the Christian understanding of the human being and his ultimate destiny. The outlines of the image of God can be seen in the human person's possessing a rational faculty, free will, creative potential, and an interior, inborn striving towards God as his Maker. The likeness is usually understood as the goal towards which the human person strives: through obedience to God and the fulfilling of His commandments, the human person is called more and more to be likened to God.

God is love and He endowed the human person with the ability to love. In creating the first people as a couple by binding the husband and the wife in a union of love, He commanded them to bear fruit and multiply. The continuation of life is impossible without love. A human being is born into this world as the fruit of the love between a man and a woman. As an infant, he is drawn towards his parents and the bonds of love unite him with them: without having yet learned to speak, he is already capable of love. Upon maturing, he enters a marriage and the life cycle is renewed in his offspring. Thus, love—the capability for which God has embedded in us—becomes the main driving force of human history: thanks to it life is conveyed from one generation to another.

White Angel. Fresco. Mileševa monastery. Serbia. 13th c.

The Visible World and the Invisible World

The Bible teaches us that, apart from the visible world, God also created the invisible world in which angels—the bodiless powers—live. It is to this world that people's souls depart after death.

The angels[7] can be both good and evil. The good angels are those who minister to God, always fulfill His will, and who are able to perform an intermediary role between God and man. The evil angels are those who have fallen away from God as a result of their pride. All their efforts are directed at resisting the will of God, at diverting people away from the true faith and observing the divine commandments.

These evil angels are called demons, and the chief among them is the **devil** or Satan.[8] It was he who first rebelled against God, taking with him many other angels, and who tempted the first people, Adam and Eve, when he appeared to them in the guise of a serpent and seduced them to disobey God (Gen 3.1–15).

God is not the creator of evil: all that He created in the beginning was "very good" (Gen 1.31). Evil was introduced into the world by the free will of rational creatures—first by the devil and demons, and then by people. Evil exists in the world only insofar as it is permitted by God and only within those limits that are determined by God.

[7] The word "angel" comes from the Greek *angelos*, meaning "messenger."

[8] The Greek word *diabolos* means "slanderer," "deceiver." The Aramaic word *satan* means "opponent."

Divine Providence

God's concern for the human person and the whole world is called **divine providence** in the language of Christian theology. This means that God gives life to every human being as well as the conditions in which to develop and grow spiritually. God does this by helping us in good deeds and directing the evil that exists in the world towards good consequences.

Providence is God's will that governs all existing things. This providence acts in a dual way. In that which is undoubtedly good, the divine will is realized without hindrance. If evil does exist in the world, then it is not as a result of God's will, but only because He has permitted it and because people hinder the divine will.[ix]

Often people say that "it is all God's will." This is incorrect. **God's will exists only for the good**; evil goes against it. In doing an evil deed willingly or unwillingly, the human person, consciously or unconsciously, goes against the will of God. Divine providence, however, acts in such a way that even people's evil deeds can be turned by God into good.

Sometimes people ask why God does not punish sinners, criminals, and bad people, why He allows evil, why He permits evil people to live among good people while still doing their evil deeds. The answer is not that God fails to notice evil or is complicit in it, but rather, the answer lies in His patience. One of the psalms states, "The Lord is compassionate and merciful, long-suffering and plenteous in mercy. His wrath will not endure until the end, neither will He be angry forever. He has not dealt with us according to our iniquities, nor rewarded us according to our sins" (Ps 102.8–10).

If God automatically cut out all manifestations of evil in human nature, He would have to deprive people of free will. This would turn people into puppets and human society into a puppet theater. God expects from every person that at each stage of his life he should consistently make the choice for good, not by being compelled to do so, but from his own free will. Evil is always abhorrent to God, yet God does not always stop evil, since He respects peoples' freedom and their right to make a choice—the right that He bestowed upon them.

At the same time, no single evil deed remains without consequences, and if a person has committed a sin and not repented, he will inevitably be punished—either in this life or in the next. In the Old Testament God describes Himself as "the Lord, the Lord God, merciful and gracious, longsuffering, and abounding in goodness and truth, keeping mercy for thousands, forgiving iniquity and transgression and sin, by no means clearing the guilty" (Ex 34.6–7).

Exile from Paradise. Fresco. Masaccio. Italy. 15th c.

God knows all things. Nothing is hidden from Him; He sees the future as the present. This does not mean, however, that everything is predetermined in the life of the human person. Christianity does not believe in predestination, fate, or destiny. God knows all of a person's deeds beforehand, both good and evil. Yet this does not mean that, when faced with the choice between good and evil, a person is predestined towards one or the other: the choice depends on our free will.

The ultimate destiny of each person is formed from the combination of the will of God, which is aimed only at good, and human will, in which good and evil are intertwined. Yet God cares for all, and even those who have consciously chosen the path of evil are not abandoned by divine providence.

The Consequences of the Fall

The consequence of the disobedience and fall of the first people was their expulsion from paradise (Gen 3.24). Since then and to this day people have remained, not in the state in which God made them, but in a different state—in the condition of **a fall from grace**. As a result of the first peoples' disobedience to God, evil entered the world, and now each person is faced with two paths: of good and of evil. God sets the human person upon the path of good and the angels help him to travel along this path. The devil and his minions, the demons, try to push humans onto the path of evil.

The Old Testament speaks of these two paths thus: "I have set before you life and death, blessing and cursing: therefore choose life, that both you and your descendants may live" (Deut 30.19). God directs this call to every person who comes into the world. Yet people, each in his own way, repeat the mistake of Adam and Eve: they listen to the whisperings of the enemy of the human race instead of listening to the voice of God.

There are philosophical currents that deny the sinful nature of the human person. They propose that all of humanity's problems are a result of people's being badly educated: if we were to explain to them where good is and where evil is, then they would choose only the good.[9]

From the perspective of Christianity, however, evil is rooted in the very nature of the fallen human person, in his heart (Mk 7.21–22). The Apostle Paul states that sin lives within a human person: "For the good that I will to do, I do not do; but the evil I will not to do, that I practice. Now if I do what I will not to do, it is no longer I who do it, but sin that dwells in me" (Rom 7.19–20). Expelling sin from within oneself and struggling with its

[9] Many philosophers from the era of the Enlightenment proceeded from this proposition.

manifestations are the highest moral tasks facing every person who believes in God. Yet we are not alone in this struggle: God Himself comes to our aid.

The Expectation of the Savior

God always struggles for the soul of each person and for his salvation. The ancients knew this and from the time of Adam lived with the hope that one of their descendants would vanquish evil and the devil. It is in this sense that the Christian tradition understands the words that God addressed to the serpent who had tempted Eve: "Because you have done this, you are cursed more than all cattle, and more than every beast of the field; on your belly you shall go, and you shall eat dust all the days of your life. And I will put enmity between you and the woman, and between your seed and her Seed; He shall bruise your head, and you shall bruise His heel" (Gen 3.14–15).

The "seed" of Eve—that is, her descendant who would win the victory over the devil and evil and who would redeem us forever "from sin, the curse and death"[x]—was Jesus Christ. The ancients lived with the expectation of His coming for many centuries, and His coming was foretold by the prophets.

Holy Prophet King David. Illuminated manuscript. Theodore Psalter. Byzantium. 12th c.

3. Jesus Christ

The Creed says of Jesus Christ: "I believe … in one Lord Jesus Christ, the Son of God, the Only-begotten, begotten of the Father before all ages: Light of light; true God of true God; begotten, not made; of one essence with the Father; by whom all things were made; who for us men and for our salvation came down from heaven, and was incarnate of the Holy Spirit and the Virgin Mary, and became man; and He was crucified for us under Pontius Pilate, and suffered, and was buried; and the third day He arose again, according to the Scriptures, and ascended into heaven, and sits at the right hand of the Father; and He shall come again with glory to judge the living and the dead; whose kingdom shall have no end."

Who is **Jesus Christ** and why does He occupy a central place in the Christian religion? Why is more than half of the text of the Creed devoted to Him? What do we know of Him and from where? Jesus called Himself the Son of Man and the Son of God (Jn 3.13–18).[10] What do these labels mean?

3.1. The Son of Man

Christ the Redeemer. Icon from the Zvenigorod Deisis tier. Andrei Rublev. Russia. *c.* 1410.

Jesus Christ is the most famous person who has ever lived on earth. There has never been another person about whom so much has been written. Books, paintings, musical compositions, and movies have been devoted to Him. He has been spoken of in sermons and written about on the internet. Moreover, churches have been built in His honor, and more than two billion people call themselves by His name. Christianity is the largest religious tradition on the planet.

[10] "Son of Man" is what Jesus Christ calls Himself most often in the Gospels. In translation from Hebrew this idiom simply means the same as "man."

The Gospels

The main source of information on Jesus Christ is the four **Gospels**—of Matthew, Mark, Luke, and John. The Gospels are eyewitness accounts of the earthly life of Jesus Christ or are based on such accounts. Of all the books in the Bible, it is the four Gospels that not only are the most read and revered but they also have the most authority in the Church. The book of the Gospels is an essential part of worship: it is brought out for veneration by the faithful who kiss it as a sign of special reverence.

From this book we learn that **Jesus Christ was a real historical person** and not an invented literary figure (as certain critics attempted to prove in the past). He was born at a concrete time in history during the reign of the Roman emperor Octavius Augustus and the Jewish king Herod the Great. He was born in Bethlehem in Judea (Mt 2.1; Lk 2.4–7).

The Birth of Jesus Christ

Jesus Christ was born in a special, supernatural manner. His mother was Mary, a young Jewish woman betrothed to a man by the name of Joseph. An angel appeared to her and announced that she would give birth to a Son whose name would be the Son of the Most High and that His kingdom would have no end. Mary asked the angel: "How can this be, since I do not know a man?" And the angel answered: "The Holy Spirit will come upon you, and the power of the Most High will overshadow you" (Lk 1.26–35).

Nativity. Icon. Andrei Rublev. Russia. 15th c.

In accordance with this Gospel narrative, the Creed states that Jesus Christ was born of **the Holy Spirit and the Virgin Mary**. The Church believes that Mary, although betrothed to Joseph, did not have marital relations with him and remained a virgin. The Church calls her "ever-virgin"—that is, she has preserved her virginity for all time.

The Four Gospels

The Gospels (from a Greek word meaning "good news") are four sacred books that are part of the New Testament.

The Gospels tell about the earthly life of Christ, His suffering, death, and Resurrection, and also reveal His teaching about salvation and the kingdom of heaven.

The Gospels were written by the Apostles Matthew, Mark, Luke, and John.

Often they are depicted next to the symbols of the winged four-faced creatures from the vision of the prophet Ezekiel (Ezek 1.1–28).

The Gospels of Matthew, Mark, and Luke are called "synoptic," since according to the events described in them, they coincide quite strongly.

1. The Gospel of Matthew

Author: the Evangelist Matthew (Levi), one of the Twelve Apostles

Date of writing: first century

The symbol of the Apostle Matthew: an angel

Christ is the promised Messiah, the Savior of Israel. Matthew constantly refers the reader to Old Testament prophecies, while emphasizing that these prophecies are fulfilled in Christ. The genealogy of Christ is from Abraham through King David.

Distinctive aspect:

Many Old Testament prophecies.

2. The Gospel of Mark

Author: the Evangelist Mark, presumably an apostle of the seventy, a disciple of the Apostle Peter

Date of writing: first century

The symbol of the Apostle Mark: a lion

The Apostle Mark wrote at the request of the Gentile Christians in Rome. His main task was to create a vivid, strong narrative about the miracles of Christ, thus emphasizing His omnipotence. In order to be correctly understood, the evangelist uses some Latin words in the narrative.

Distinctive aspect:

The shortest of the Gospels.

Authenticity of the Gospels

For ancient texts, all four Gospels have an unprecedented number of manuscript copies. They were unconditionally accepted by the Christian communities of the first and second centuries. The oldest surviving manuscripts of the gospel texts date back to the beginning of the second century.

The oldest complete list of the books of the New Testament is part of the Codex Sinaïticus (fourth century). The final canon of the New Testament, the core of which is the four Gospels, was fixed at the local Council of Laodicea in 360. It was confirmed at the Sixth Ecumenical Council in Constantinople in 680.

3. The Gospel of Luke

Author: The Evangelist Luke, presumably an apostle of the seventy, a disciple of the Apostle Paul

Date of writing: first century

The symbol of the Apostle Luke: an ox

Christ came into the world to save not only the Jews, but the entire human race. Luke cites the earthly genealogy of the Savior, tracing it backwards from Jesus to the first man, Adam. In the Gospel of Luke there are episodes and parables that show the merciful attitude of Christ towards the Gentiles.

Distinctive aspect:

An abundance of parables.

4. The Gospel of John

Author: The Evangelist John (the Theologian), one of the twelve apostles, beloved disciple of Christ

Date of writing: first century

The symbol of the Apostle John: an eagle

A supplement to the first three gospels. It most fully represents the conversations of Christ with the Jews, and his annual pilgrimages to Jerusalem.

Distinctive aspects:

Revealing the divine dignity of Christ.
Contains lengthy discourses of Christ.
Includes events not mentioned by other authors.
The last of the four to be written.

The name "Jesus," given to the Infant at His birth, means "the Lord saves" in Hebrew. The Greek word "Christ" is used for Jesus many times in the New Testament and means "the Anointed One."[11]

Supernatural signs accompanied the birth of Jesus Christ: the angels announced His birth to the shepherds (Lk 2.8–18), and the Magi from the east, led by a mysterious star, came in order to worship Him (Mt 2.1–12).

On the eighth day after His birth, the infant Jesus was circumcised according to the Jewish law (Lk 2.21), and on the fortieth day Mary and Joseph brought Him to the Temple in Jerusalem to dedicate Him to the Lord. There they were greeted by the righteous elder Symeon, who foretold that Jesus would become a "light to bring revelation to the gentiles" and the glory of the people of Israel (Lk 2.23–33).

Meeting of the Lord. Bas-relief.

The Baptism of Jesus and the Beginning of His Preaching

In the fifteenth year of the rule of the Roman emperor Tiberius a prophet appeared on the banks of the river Jordan. He not only called upon people to repent of their sins, but he also performed a ritual of baptism by immersing them in the waters of the Jordan. This act was a sign of purification from their sins. All four evangelists, as well as other historical sources (for example, the first-century Jewish Roman historian Flavius Josephus) testify to this prophet, who in church tradition is called **John the Baptist** or John the Forerunner.

John said to the people that came to him: "I baptize you with water unto repentance, but He who is coming

[11] *Christos* is the Greek translation of the Hebrew word *Mashiach*, which comes into English as "Messiah."

after me is more powerful than I, whose sandals I am not worthy to carry. He will baptize you with the Holy Spirit and fire." When Jesus came to the Jordan to receive Baptism from John, the latter tried at first to forbid Him and said: "I need to be baptized by You, and are You coming to me?" But Jesus answered him: "Permit it to be so now; for thus it is fitting for us to fulfill all righteousness." Then John allowed Jesus to be baptized. And when Jesus emerged from the waters, "The heavens were opened to Him and He saw the Spirit of God descending like a dove and alighting upon Him. And suddenly a voice came from heaven, saying, 'This is My beloved Son, in whom

Epiphany. Mosaic, St Mark's Basilica, Venice, Italy. 13th c.

I am well pleased'" (Mt 3.11–17; Mk 1.9–11; Lk 3.21–22). By this time Jesus was about thirty years old (Lk 3.23).

After His Baptism, He withdrew into the wilderness where He spent forty days without food and water. There He was tempted by the devil, but He vanquished all temptations and emerged victorious from this battle with the devil (Mt 4.1–11; Mk 1.12–13; Lk 4.1–13).

Jesus began His preaching with the very same words that John the Baptist addressed to the people: "Repent, for the kingdom of heaven is at hand" (Mt 3.2; 4.17). Very soon a group of disciples and followers gathered around Jesus, from whom He chose twelve to be apostles (Mk 3.14, Lk 6.13). Crowds of people followed Him, attracted by His miracles and His teachings.

The Miracles of Jesus Christ

The **miracles** are the aspect of the ministry of Jesus Christ that drew the greatest attention from those around Him during His life. Already at the very beginning of His preaching in Galilee "His fame went throughout all Syria; and they brought to Him all sick people who were afflicted with various diseases and torments, and those who were demon-possessed, epileptics, and paralytics; and He healed them. Great multitudes followed Him—from Galilee, and from Decapolis, Jerusalem, Judea, and beyond the Jordan" (Mt 4.24–25). In time His fame only grew, while some of the people whom He healed, including women, became a part of His group of disciples (Lk 8.2–3).

The stories of the miracles performed by Jesus upon entering his public ministry comprise an important part of the Gospel narratives. In total, we find in the Gospels more than thirty complete stories of the miracles of Jesus (not including the short mentions of various supernatural events that accompanied His life and ministry). Among them there are numerous healings, the expulsion of demons from the possessed, raising three

Appearance of Christ on the shores of Lake Tiberias. Duccio di Buoninsegna. Italy. 1255–1318.

people from the dead, several events testifying to Jesus' power over nature (walking on water, the calming of a storm, and cursing of the fig tree), and a number of other supernatural events (the transformation of water into wine, the feeding of the five thousand and the seven thousand with a small number of loaves, two miraculous catches of fish).

As regards the total number of the miracles performed by Jesus, they cannot be subject to calculation: there may be hundreds if not thousands of healings. This is witnessed by the many places in the Gospels where it is evident that the miracles He performed and the expulsion of demons bore a mass character.[12]

[12] See: Mt 4.23–24; 8.16–17; 9.35; 12.15; 14.35–36; 15.30–31; 19.2; 21.14; Mk 1.32–34, 39; 3.10–11; 6.54–56; Lk 4.40–41; 6.17–19; 6.54–56; 7.21; Jn 20.30.

Miracles and Faith

The Gospels do not contain a single episode where Jesus refused to heal somebody. But He refused to perform miracles in those instances when a sign was demanded of Him to demonstrate His power. He did not want to perform any of the miracles that the devil expected of Him when he tempted Jesus in the wilderness. He refused the Pharisees and the Sadducees when they asked Him to show them a sign from heaven (Mt 16.1–4; Mk 8.11–12).

The Pharisees demanded miracles supposedly in order to believe in Him, yet it was faith, as He taught, which ought to be the sole condition for performing a miracle: **miracles are the result of faith, not its cause.** Jesus said to His disciples: "If you have faith as a mustard seed, you will say to this mountain, 'Move from here to there,' and it will move; and nothing will be impossible for you" (Mt 17.20). For the one who believes in God, nothing is impossible. A miracle may be a reality of his life—as evident and indisputable as the surrounding world.

Jesus many times required belief from those who were healed, or He tested their belief. He asked the blind men who begged Him to heal them: "Do you believe that I am able to do this?" (Mt 9.28). He also often noted the saving power of the faith of the one who had been healed: "Your faith has made you well" (Mt 9.22; Mk 10.52); "O woman, great is your faith! Let it be to you as you desire" (Mt 15.28; Lk 7.50); "Daughter, your faith has made you well; go in peace, and be healed of your affliction" (Mk 5.34; Lk 8.48); "Get up and go on your way; your faith has made you well" (Lk 17.19); "Receive your sight; your faith has made you well" (Lk 18.42).

Not all of those who begged Jesus to heal them had steadfast faith: some hesitated and doubted and were still halfway between doubt and belief. But the Lord helped them to be strengthened in faith. One man's son had suffered from severe seizures since childhood and the man brought him to Jesus and said: "If you can do anything, have compassion on us and help us." Jesus answered him: "If you can believe, all things can be done for to him who believes" And the father of the boy exclaimed with tears: "Lord, I believe; help my unbelief" (Mk 9.17–27). In healing the boy from a serious illness, Jesus simultaneously healed his father from the spiritual infirmity of unbelief.

The Transfiguration of the Lord

A special place among the miracles of Jesus Christ is occupied by the **Transfiguration**, when "Jesus took Peter, James, and John his brother, led them up on a high mountain by themselves; and He was transfigured before them. His face shone like the sun, and His clothes became as white as the light. And behold, Moses and Elijah appeared to them, talking with Him. Then Peter answered and said to Jesus, 'Lord, it is good for us to be here; if You wish, let us make here three tabernacles: one for You, one for Moses, and one for Elijah.' While he was still speaking, behold, a bright cloud overshadowed them; and suddenly a voice came out of the cloud, saying, 'This is My beloved Son, in whom I am well pleased. Hear Him!'" (Mt 17.1–5; cf. Mk 9.1–7; Lk 9.28–35).

Transfiguration. Icon. Russia. End of 15th c.

As a result of this miracle, the divine nature of Jesus, which had been concealed beneath the veil of human flesh, was revealed to His disciples. The glory of God that abided in Jesus was made manifest in a special visible manner. The light that Jesus possessed according to His divine nature was made manifest.

According to the teaching of St Gregory Palamas (fourteenth century), the light that the disciples contemplated on the mount of the Transfiguration was not a conventional physical light, but a special action of God through which God revealed His presence. The divine light changes and transforms the human person and those who saw it did not "simply see with the eyes of sense, but with eyes transformed by the power of the Holy Spirit."[xi]

The Parables of Jesus Christ

Jesus is presented in the Gospels as the **Teacher**—an itinerant preacher wandering from one city to another and speaking to people of the kingdom of God. In His speech Jesus often used images and comparisons taken from everyday life or from the world of nature. His speech was striking, colorful, and poetic.

Many of His teachings take the form of **parables**—short metaphorical narratives that convey spiritual and moral truths. The Gospels contain more than thirty such narratives. The use of parables as the basic form of transmitting spiritual and moral truths was so characteristic of Jesus that the evangelists specially noted it: "All these things Jesus spoke to the multitude in parables; and without a parable He did not speak to them" (Mt 13.34); "With many such parables He spoke the word to them, as they were able to hear it; but without a parable He did not speak to them" (Mk 4.33–34). When Jesus ceased to speak in parables this even evoked surprise: "See, now You are speaking plainly, and using no figure of speech!" (Jn 16.29).

The Return of the Prodigal Son. Detail. Rembrandt Harmenszoon van Rijn. Dutch. 1668.

The key to understanding the parables is faith. This makes Jesus' parables akin to His miracles. For those whose hearts have hardened, who do not see with their eyes and hear with their ears, the meaning of the parables remains hidden (Mt 13.13; Mk 4.12; Lk 8.10; Jn 12.40). As Jesus' miracles did not convince the scribes and the

Pharisees of the truth of His teaching, so too His teaching set forth in the parables did not convince them that He was the Messiah sent from God. And, by contrast, because they came to believe, many witnesses to Jesus' miracles and many of those who heard His parables came to understand His messianic role.

The parables of Jesus possess an unsurpassed value in that they help the human person to understand God better, help him to draw closer to God, to love Him. In these parables God is present as sovereign master who enjoys absolute power over all His subjects: He gives to each as much as He considers necessary, and then demands from each an account of how what has been received was spent (Mt 22.7). At the same time, He reveals Himself as the long-suffering father of great mercy who is ready to embrace a repentant sinner (Lk 15.20). God loves each human being as His own creature and child, and many of the parables—each in its own way—reveal this truth.

The parables, moreover, speak of the Only-begotten Son of God. In them He is manifested not only as a wise Teacher, but also as the Good Shepherd (Jn 10.1–16) who goes to seek out the lost sheep, finds it, carries it back on His shoulders, and rejoices in the fact that it has been found (Lk 15.4–6). He is shown to be the One whom God sent into the vineyard in order to

The Parables of Christ

A parable in the New Testament is a short instructive story or aphorism in which Christ reveals the meaning of the Good News through simple images familiar to any listener.

Themes of the parables:

- God and man (grey)
- the kingdom of heaven (orange)
- the Last Judgment (purple)
- relationships with neighbors (green)

Parables relating to the Galilean period of ministry of the Savior

	Parable	The Gospel of Matthew	of Luke	of Mark
God and man	The bridegroom and His guests	Mt 9.14–15	Lk 5.33–35	Mk 2.18–20
God and man	New cloth on old garments and new wine in old wineskins	Mt 9.16–17	Lk 5.36–39	Mk 2.21–22
God and man	The salt of the earth, the light of the world, the city on top of the hill, and the candle under the basket	Mt 5.13–16	Lk 8.16, 11.33 Lk 14.34–35	Mk 4.21–25 Mk 9.50
God and man	The house built on the rock	Mt 7.24–27	Lk 647–49	
God and man	The children in the marketplace		Lk 7.32	
God and man; the kingdom of heaven; the Last Judgment; relationships with neighbors	The unmerciful servant	Mt 18.21–35	Lk 7.36–50	
the kingdom of heaven	A kingdom divided, the house of the strong man, and other short parables	Mt 12.24–29	Lk 11.17–22	Mk 3.23–27
God and man; the kingdom of heaven	The sower	Mt 13.1–23	Lk 8.4–15	Mk 4.1–20
the kingdom of heaven; the Last Judgment	The wheat and the tares	Mt 13.24–43		
the kingdom of heaven	The seed that grows unnoticed			Mk 4.26–29
the kingdom of heaven	The mustard seed	Mt 13.31–32	Lk 13.18–19	Mk 4.30–32
the kingdom of heaven	The leaven	Mt 13.33–35	Lk 13.20–21	Mk 4.33–34
God and man; the kingdom of heaven	The treasure in a field	Mt 13.44		
God and man; the kingdom of heaven	The pearl of great price	Mt 13.45–46		
the kingdom of heaven; the Last Judgment	The net	Mt 13.47–50		
relationships with neighbors	The two blind men	Mt 15.14	Lk 6.39–40	

The parable of the wheat and the tares

Parables told by Christ on the way to Jerusalem

The parable	The Gospel of Matthew	of Luke	of John
The good samaritan		Lk 10.30–37	
The friend at midnight		Lk 11.5–8	
The rich fool		Lk 12.16–21	
The watchful servants		Lk 12.35–40	
The faithful and unfaithful servants		Lk 12.42–48	
The good shepherd			Jn 10.1–18
The barren fig tree		Lk 13.6–9	
The proud guests at the feast		Lk 14.7–11	
The wedding feast		Lk 14.16–24	
The tower builder		Lk 14.28–30	
The king preparing for war		Lk 14.31–32	
The lost sheep	Mt 18.10–14	Lk 15.1–7	
The lost coin		Lk 15.8–10	
The prodigal son		Lk 15.11–32	
The unjust steward		Lk 16.1–12	
Serving two masters		Lk 16.13	
The rich man and Lazarus		Lk 16.19–31	
The unprofitable servants		Lk 17.7–10	
The persistent widow		Lk 18.1–8	
The publican and the Pharisee		Lk 18.9–14	
The laborers in the vineyard	Mt 20.1–16		
The talents and minas	Mt 25.14–30	Lk 19.11–27	

Parables told by Christ in the last days in Jerusalem

The parable	The Gospel of Matthew	of Luke	of Mark
The two sons	Mt 21.28–32		
The wicked tenants	Mt 21.33–41	Lk 20.9–19	Mk 12.1–9
The marriage feast	Mt 22.1–14		
The barren fig tree	Mt 24.32–36	Lk 21.29–33	Mk 13.28–32
The householder and the thief	Mt 24.43		Mk 13.32–37
The wise steward	Mt 24.45–51		
The ten virgins	Mt 25.1–13		
Ten talents and the minas	Mt 25.13–30		
The Last Judgement	Mt 25.31–46		

The parable of the wicked tenants

gather the fruits, and who was obedient to the will of the Father at the price of His own life (Mt 21.33–41).

Finally, the parables speak of how we are to build up our relationships with our neighbors. We are called upon to forgive as the father forgave his prodigal son, as God forgives debtors (Mt 18.27); to respond to another's pain in the same way that the Good Samaritan responded to the affliction of the man who fell prey to robbers (Lk 10.30–37); to love as the one to whom much has been forgiven loves (Lk 7.41–47); to see people through the eyes of God by peering into the depths of their soul and seeing in them the image of God.

The Kingdom of Heaven

The basic theme of the teachings and parables of Jesus was the **kingdom of heaven**, or the kingdom of God. Nowhere does Jesus give a definition of the kingdom of heaven, but He reveals its essence through an entire series of images, comparisons, and parables.

He sometimes begins His parables with the question: "What is the kingdom of God like? And to what shall I compare it?" (Lk 13.18); or with the answers to these questions: "The kingdom of heaven is like a mustard seed. … The kingdom of heaven is like leaven. … The kingdom of heaven is like treasure hidden in a field. … The kingdom of heaven is like a merchant. … The kingdom of heaven is like a dragnet" (Mt 13.31, 33, 44, 45, 47).

In the preaching of Jesus Christ, the kingdom of heaven is an all-embracing concept: it is impossible to reduce it either to the present or to the future, either to earthly reality or to eternity; it has no concrete earthly outlines, nor a concrete verbal expression; it cannot be localized either in time or space; it is addressed not to the here-and-now and the external, but to the heavenly, the future, and that which is inwards. The kingdom of heaven is a reality that in an unseen way permeates human life and relationships; it shines through various objects and appearances that surround people; it endows life with meaning and justification.

Jesus speaks of the kingdom of heaven as an inner experience of the human person. Once the Pharisees asked Him when the kingdom of God would come and He replied to them: "The kingdom of God does not come with observation; nor will they say, 'See here!' or 'See there!' For indeed, the kingdom of God is within you" (Lk 17.20–21).

In announcing the advent of the kingdom of God, Jesus reveals to people a new quality of life, the center of which is God. Jesus' message of the kingdom of God, however, is not confined to the call to obey God—otherwise it would in no way differ from the message brought to people by the Old Testament prophets. They, too, spoke of the necessity of repentance, the transformation of one's way of thinking and way of life, of God's action in history, of His presence among people. The God of the Old Testament is also the Living God, yet abiding remotely from people in the heavens, beyond the clouds, and revealing His glory in thunder and lightning.

The radical newness of Jesus' message of the kingdom of heaven lies in the notion that He Himself has brought this kingdom down from the heavens to earth. And not only the kingdom: He makes manifest to people the heavenly God in opening up to them the hitherto invisible and unknown, hidden and inaccessible divine countenance.[13] The kingdom of heaven becomes not only a reality of the future, but also a new dimension in peoples' lives here and now, on earth and in time.

The Apostle Paul calls this dimension "eternal life in Christ Jesus our Lord" (Rom 6.23). It is not merely life in God, but precisely life through Jesus Christ. It is eternal not because it begins for people after death: it already begins here, from the moment when one

[13] The expression "divine countenance" in the present *Catechism* is used in a metaphorical sense in the same way that the Old Testament speaks of the hands, feet, and eyes of God.

believes in Christ and becomes His disciple, but it continues in eternity.

In preaching the kingdom of God, Jesus reveals Himself to people. At the same time, He opens up to them the way to God. Of Himself He states: "I am the way, the truth, and the life. No one comes to the Father except through Me" (Jn 14.6).

The kingdom of heaven is inseparable from Jesus' person, from His cause, His preaching, and His witness. Ultimately, the kingdom of heaven is revealed not so much through Jesus' teachings as through His redemptive sacrifice, the story of which concludes each of the Gospels.

Jesus' Opponents

All four Gospels speak of the development of an acute conflict between Jesus and those who represented the religious elite of the people of Israel at that time: the high priests, Pharisees, and scribes. This conflict arose shortly after Jesus appeared to preach and in time became deeper.

The disputes between Jesus and His opponents touched upon the essence of religious life. What is faith? What sort of worship does God demand? The **scribes and Pharisees** believed that faith was the totality of rules fixed in the written law and oral tradition that one ought to observe unswervingly.

Pharisees. "Christ Accused by the Pharisees," detail. Duccio di Buoninsegna. Italy. 1308.

But as there were too many rules, the Pharisees created an entire system of exceptions that allowed them to violate these rules. The Pharisees believed that God should be worshipped only in Jerusalem and that the Hebrew people are chosen and predestined for salvation. The Samaritans disputed with them, believing that God should not be worshipped in Jerusalem, but on Mount Gerizim. These disputes occasionally led to armed conflict and murder.

The Resurrection of Lazarus. Fresco. Giotto di Bondone. Italy. 1304–1306.

Jesus, in contrast, said that "the hour is coming when you will worship the Father neither on this mountain nor in Jerusalem. You worship what you do not know; we know what we worship, for salvation is of the Jews. But the hour is coming, and is now, when the true worshipers will worship the Father in spirit and truth, for the Father is seeking such to worship Him" (Jn 4.21–23).

He taught that the worship of God cannot be reduced to the scrupulous observance of a sum of regulations, even if they are sanctified by God's authority. The heart of true spiritual life consists of seeking out the kingdom of heaven: all of a person's strivings should be directed to this one goal. Jesus called people to repentance—to an inner rebirth that in no way is confined to fulfilling certain external rules.

The Law of Moses and Disputes on the Sabbath

Often disputes between Jesus and His opponents touched upon the concrete ordinances of the **Law of Moses**.[14] One of the commandments of this law states: "Remember the

[14] We conventionally call "the Law of Moses" the collection of ordinances and laws contained in the Pentateuch—the first five books of the Bible, especially in the Books of Exodus, Leviticus, Numbers, and Deuteronomy.

Sabbath day, to keep it holy. Six days you shall labor and do all your work, but the seventh day is a Sabbath to the Lord your God" (Ex 20. 8–10). The meaning of the commandment was that man was to devote one of the days of the week—the Sabbath—to God in keeping His earthly affairs and concerns to a minimum. But the Pharisees turned this commandment into a dogma: they established the maximum distance a person could tread on the Sabbath and many other limitations concerning the Sabbath, and by these practices, the Pharisees believed, a person could please God.

The Healing of the Ten Lepers. Fresco. Serbia. 15th c.

Yet Jesus stated that "the Sabbath was made for man, and not man for the Sabbath" (Mk 2.27). That which is a means should not be turned into an end. The external rules are merely the means of attaining inner goals. It was to these goals that His preaching was addressed. He permitted His disciples, as they went through the corn fields on the Sabbath, to pluck the ears of grain and eat them, something the Pharisees did not permit. In response to the Pharisees' indignation, Jesus said of Himself: "The Son of Man is Lord even of the Sabbath" (Mt 12.1–8).

Jesus performed many healings on the Sabbath—and not because He purposely aimed to violate the commandment to rest on the Sabbath, but because on the Sabbath He would go to the synagogues where crowds of people had gathered, many of whom turned to Him for healing.

Once He healed a woman who for eighteen years had been bent down and could not straighten herself up. Seeing this, the ruler of the synagogue, "Answered with indignation because Jesus had healed on the Sabbath, and he said to the crowd, 'There are six days on which men ought to work; therefore come and be healed on them, and not on the Sabbath day.' The Lord answered him and said, 'Hypocrite! Does not each one of you on the Sabbath loose his ox or donkey

The healing of the bent over woman. Fresco. Serbia. 15th c.

from the stall, and lead it away to water it? So ought not this woman, being a daughter of Abraham, whom Satan has bound—think of it—for eighteen years, be loosed from this bond on the Sabbath?'" (Lk 13.10–16).

The Pharisees believed that good could be accomplished only according to schedule and even the order of performing miracles should be clearly regulated. For them, good was not an end in itself: the main thing was ritual, the observance of rules, the following of the Law of Moses and the "tradition of the elders." Yet for Jesus the focus of attention was the living person—the one who encountered Him on the road or at home or in the synagogue, and who was in need of help here and now, and not at some point in the future. Jesus did not pass by such people. If they turned to Him, He immediately performed healings, and the Sabbath was no hindrance to Him.

Disputes on Purity and Impurity

The Pharisees considered themselves to be separate from ordinary people (the word "Pharisee" itself means "separate"), enjoying a special proximity to God. Their main concern was not to be defiled by contact with something or someone unclean. The Old Testament lists unclean people and objects, and the Pharisees added numerous clarifying details to them. According to the evangelist Mark, "The Pharisees and all the Jews do not eat unless they wash their hands in a special way, thus observing the tradition of the elders. When they come from the marketplace, they do not eat unless they wash. And there are many other things which they have received and hold, like the washing of cups, pitchers, copper vessels, and couches" (Mk 7.3–4).

Yet Jesus taught that the source of impurity and sin is not outside a person, but within him. He said, "There is nothing that enters a man from outside which can defile him; but the things which come out of him, those are the things that defile a man. … For from within, out of the heart of men, proceed evil thoughts, adulteries, fornications, murders, thefts, covetousness, wickedness, deceit, lewdness, an evil eye, blasphemy, pride, foolishness. All these evil things come from within and defile a man" (Mk 7.15, 21–23).

Jesus, who was forgiving of human weaknesses, did not disdain conversation with sinful women (Lk 7.36–50) and adulteresses (Jn 8.3–11), and ate with publicans[15] and sinners (Mt 9.11; Mk 2.16). Yet He was severe with regard to the Pharisees, harshly denouncing their sanctimoniousness and calling them a "generation of vipers," "hypocrites," "blind guides," and likened them to "whitewashed tombs, which indeed appear beautiful outwardly, but inside are full of dead men's bones and all uncleanness" (Mt 23.13–27).

The conflict between Jesus and the Pharisees reached its high point when He raised Lazarus from the dead after he had been buried in a cave for four days. After this, the high priests and Pharisees resolved to kill Him (Jn 11.43–53). Their resolve held out over a number of days, and the ideal opportunity presented itself when Jesus triumphantly entered Jerusalem on the foal of an ass to the exalted cries of the crowd. Then "all the city was moved, saying, 'Who is this?' So the multitudes said, 'This is Jesus, the prophet from Nazareth in Galilee'" (Mt 21.6–11). And the high priests and the Pharisees gave "a command, that if anyone knew where He was, he should report it, that they might seize Him" (Jn 11.57).

[15] Publicans were Israelites who collected taxes for the Romans, and thus were seen as collaborators with the occupying power.

The Last Supper. Icon. Athens, Greece. 12th c.

The Last Supper

In the night before His arrest Jesus held His last meal with the disciples, subsequently known as the **Last Supper**. We know of this from all four of the Gospels.

According to the narrative of Matthew, Mark, and Luke, the Last Supper was a Passover meal,[16] at which "Jesus took bread, blessed and broke it, and gave it to the disciples and said, 'Take, eat; this is My body.' Then He took the cup, and gave thanks, and gave it to them, saying, 'Drink from it, all of you. For this is My blood of the new covenant, which is shed for many for the remission of sins. But I say to you, I will not drink of this fruit of the vine from now on until that day when I drink it new with you in My Father's kingdom'" (Mt 26.26–29; Mk 14.22–25). He commanded His disciples: "Do this in remembrance of Me" (Lk 22.19). It is this commandment that forms the basis of the most important of the Church's sacraments—the Eucharist.

[16] The Jewish Passover was a feast day established to commemorate the liberation of the people of Israel from Egyptian captivity. On this day it was customary to eat a specially prepared Paschal lamb with unleavened bread.

According to the Gospel of John, before the supper Jesus removed His upper garments, "poured water into a basin and began to wash the disciples' feet, and to wipe them with the towel with which He was girded." (Jn 13.4–5).

He then gave His last teaching, a significant part of which is devoted to love: "Little children, I shall be with you a little while longer. You will seek Me; and as I said to the Jews, 'Where I am going, you cannot come,' so now I say to you. A new commandment I give to you, that you love one another; as I have loved you, that you also love one another. By this all will know that you are My disciples, if you have love for one another. … As the Father loved Me, I also have loved you; abide in My love. If you keep My commandments, you will abide in My love, just as I have kept My Father's commandments and abide in His love. … This is My commandment, that you love one another as I have loved you" (Jn 13.33–35; 15.9–10, 12).

As He left the world, these words became the testament that Jesus bequeathed through His disciples to all subsequent generations.

Stone of the Agony in the Garden of Gethsemane.

The Suffering, Death, and Burial of Jesus

Jesus repeatedly **foretold His death**. He knew that He had come into this world to "give His life a ransom for many" (Mt 20.28). He went to His death in obedience to the will of His Father.

Jesus was afraid of death in a human way. On the night before His arrest He said to His disciples: "'My soul is exceedingly sorrowful, even to death. Stay here and watch with Me.' He went a little farther and fell on His face, and prayed, saying, 'O My Father, if it is possible, let this cup pass from Me; nevertheless, not as I will, but as You will'" (Mt 26.38–39). Also, "His sweat became like great drops of blood falling down to the ground"(Lk

Kiss of Judah. Bas-relief. Bremen Cathedral. Germany. 14th c.

22.44). At the same time, knowing that death was inevitable, He meekly accepted the will of the Father. **His obedience to the Father** was absolute: He "humbled Himself and became obedient to the point of death, even the death of the cross" (Phil 2.8). Jesus was condemned to death by the Jewish Sanhedrin[17] and crucified at the order of the prefect Pontius Pilate.[18] At His trial He did not seek to justify Himself. He silently endured the accusations and mockery and was subjected to scourging.

Jesus was crucified upon a cross. He died in terrible agony. When the Roman soldiers nailed Him to the cross, He prayed: "Father, forgive them; for they do not know what they do" (Lk 23.34). On the cross He cried out to His Father: "My God, My God, why have You forsaken Me?" (Mt 27.46; Mk 15.34; quoting Ps 21.1).

[17] The Sanhedrin was the supreme court consisting of the high priest and seventy judges.

[18] Judea at the time was ruled by a Roman governor occupying the post of prefect (later this post would be called the procurator).

Christ Carrying the Cross. El Greco. Spain. 1577.

The Church believes that Jesus was never for a moment abandoned by God the Father, but, in order to save people, He had to experience the harshest of sufferings, not only of the body, but also of the soul. Jesus voluntarily took upon Himself the cup of suffering and was to drink it to the bottom. And the bottom of human suffering and the greatest affliction that can befall a human being is to be abandoned by God—the silence of God and His seeming absence.

Jesus' suffering on the cross manifested to the highest degree His solidarity with all those who suffer—including those who, in suffering, doubt God's presence, raise their voice up against God, and despair. Jesus does not raise up His voice and rebel, neither does He doubt nor hesitate, yet the unbearable physical pain that He endured is multiplied in the moral agony that He felt as the Man who has been left alone with the terror of agony before death. He was not abandoned by God, yet He had to go through the experience of being abandoned by God for "He had to be made like His brethren, that He might be a merciful and faithful High Priest in things pertaining to God, to make propitiation for the sins of the people. For in that He Himself has suffered, being tempted, He is able to aid those who are tempted" (Heb 2.17–18).

For Jesus, God remained the Father even at the moment when He was subjected to terrible afflictions. As the evangelist Luke testifies, the last words Jesus uttered on the cross were: "Father, into Your hands I commit My spirit" (Lk 23.46). And having said this, He surrendered His spirit.

The Crucifixion. Icon. Russia. 15th c.

Jesus' body was removed from the cross and buried in a cave, in accordance with custom. On the day of the Sabbath, which coincided with the Jewish feast of the Passover, His body lay in the tomb, while the women who were His followers "rested on the Sabbath according to the commandment" (Lk 23.56).

Pietà. Michelangelo di Lodovico Buonarroti Simoni. Italy. 1499.

The Resurrection

Early in the morning on the first day of the week the women came to Jesus' tomb in order to anoint His body with spices. They saw that the tomb was empty and the angels announced to them the news that **Jesus had risen** (Mt 28.2–7; Lk 24.4–7). After this, two of the disciples—Peter and John—ran to the tomb and saw in it only the burial garments that Jesus had left (Jn 20. 3–10). Then the risen Jesus appeared to Mary Magdalene[19] immediately by the tomb (Mk 16.9; Jn 20.11–18), to the other women when they departed from the tomb (Mt 28.9–10), to two disciples on the road to Emmaus (Mk 16. 12–13), and to a group of disciples (Mk 16.14; Lk. 24.36–50; Jn 20.19–25). Eight days later Jesus again appeared to the disciples (Jn 20.26–29), and then on many occasions He appeared to various groups of His followers (Jn 21.1–23; 1 Cor 15.5–7).

Finally, appearing to the disciples on a mountain in Galilee, He said to them: "All authority has been given to Me in heaven and on earth. Go therefore and make disciples of all the nations, baptizing them in the name of the Father and of the Son and of the Holy Spirit, teaching them to observe all things that I have commanded you; and lo, I am with you always, even to the end of the age" (Mt 28.18–20). After this, "He was received up into heaven and sat down at the right hand of God" (Mk 16.19).

The Myrrh-bearers at the Tomb. Icon. Russia. 1497.

The Resurrection of Jesus Christ was the most important news that the apostles—Jesus' disciples chosen by Him for the continuation of His ministry—brought into the world. It was the basic theme of their

[19] Mary Magdalene is one of the female disciples of Christ. Of all the women who followed Him she is mentioned in the Gospels the most often (Mt 27.56, 61; 28.1; Mk 15.40, 47; 16.1, 9; Lk 8.2; 24.10; Jn 19.25; 20.1, 11–18).

preaching. The meaning of this fact was so evident and absolute for the early Church that the Apostle Paul could say when addressing the Corinthians: "If Christ is not risen, then our preaching is empty and your faith is also empty" (1 Cor 15.14).

The Resurrection of Jesus Christ remains today the heart of the Christian faith. It is precisely around this event that the entire theology of the Christian Church is centered. All of the annual cycle of feasts in the Church's liturgical calendar is tied to Christ's Resurrection, which is called the "feast of feasts" and "triumph of triumphs."

3.2. The Son of God

For the Christian Church, Jesus Christ is not merely a human being. He is the incarnate God. It is the belief in Jesus Christ as God and Savior that sets Christians apart from non-Christians.

Jesus—the Only-Begotten Son of God

The Church believes that Jesus Christ is the **Only-begotten Son of God**. The Gospel of John begins with the words: "In the beginning was the Word, and the Word was with God, and the Word was God. He was in the beginning with God. … In Him was life, and the life was the light of men. And the light shines in the darkness, and the darkness did not comprehend it" (Jn 1.1–2, 4–5). The Word here is understood to be the "Only-begotten Son, who is in the bosom of the Father," who reveals to the world God who cannot be seen (Jn 1.18).

The creed affirms that the Son of God is born, but not made: unlike human beings and angels, He is not a creature of God, but abides from all eternity in unity with the Father. All of God's creatures are distinguished from God in essence, whereas the Son of God is "consubstantial [or 'one in essence'] with the Father"—that is, the Father and the Son possess a single divine essence.

According to His divine nature He is begotten of the Father—that is, born not in time but in eternity. The Son is equal to the Father and always abides with the Father: there was never a time when the Father was not with the Son. As a human being, though, He was incarnate at a definite historical moment from the Holy Spirit and the Virgin Mary.

Jesus—the God-man

The Only-begotten Son of God, the Lord Jesus Christ, is the **God-man**—that is, God and a human being at the same time. He is not a half-man and a half-god, but perfect (that is, complete and entire) man and perfect God.

In becoming man, the Son of God made those who believe in Him the children of His heavenly Father and became for them their kinsman and brother.[xii]

Christ in Majesty. Icon. Russia. *c.* 1500.

In His person Jesus Christ united time and eternity, heaven and earth, the human and the divine. In His human nature He was akin to us in all things apart from sin: like other people, He ate and drank (Mt. 9.10–13), could be surprised (Mt 8.10; Lk 7.9), became tired (Jn 4.6), slept (Mt 8.24; Mk 4.38), became angry (Mk 3.5), was indignant (Mk 10.14), rejoiced (Lk 10.21), wept (Jn 11.35), was sorrowful, was horrified, and endured heaviness of soul (Mt 26.37–38; Mk 14.33–34). Yet all manifestations of human nature within Him were without sinfulness.

The Two Natures of Christ

Two natures—divine and human—are united in Jesus Christ "unconfusedly, unchangeably, indivisibly, inseparably."[20] This means that the two natures in Christ do not merge into one so that each of them would constitute a

[20] This is the definition of the Council of Chalcedon (NPNF^2 14.264).

new nature; one nature is not engulfed by the other; one nature is not substituted for the other when unified. At the same time, they are not separated one from the other and are not divided after they have been united at the moment of conception from the Holy Spirit.

Jesus Christ is a single undivided person in whom the divine and human natures are united in a harmonious and inextricable way. This is the reason why Christian theology does not separate the eternal Son of God from the man Jesus, who was born in time. And, although the Virgin Mary gave birth to Jesus in human fashion, she is called the **Theotokos** because the eternal Son of God and the man Jesus, who was born in time, are one and the same person.

Jesus washing the apostles' feet. Illuminated manuscripts. Byzantium. 11th c.

Jesus—Lord and God

The Church bestows upon Jesus Christ the same names with which she honors the heavenly Father: **Lord** and **God**. These two names in relation to Jesus were uttered for the first time by the Apostle Thomas, who was not present at the first appearance of the risen Christ to the disciples. When they told him that they had seen the Lord, he replied: "'Unless I see in His hands the print of the nails, and put my finger into the print of the nails, and put my hand into His side, I will not believe.' And after eight days His disciples were again inside, and Thomas with them. Jesus came, the doors being shut, and stood in the midst, and said, 'Peace to you!' Then He said to Thomas, 'Reach your finger here, and look at My hands; and reach your hand here, and put it into My side. Do not be unbelieving, but believing.' And Thomas answered and said to Him, 'My Lord and my God!'" (Jn 20.25–28).

The Creed calls Jesus "one Lord" and "true God of true God." This emphasizes the equal dignity of the Father and the Son.

The words of the Creed "by whom all things were made" point toward the participation of the Son of God in the creation of the world and the human person. "All things were made through Him, and without Him nothing was made that was made," states the Gospel of John (Jn 1.3), while the Epistle to the Hebrews speaks of the Son by whom God "made the worlds" (Heb 1.2). The Church believes that when God the Father created the world, the Son of God participated in the divine creative process.

Jesus—Light of Light

The Creed calls Jesus "Light of Light." God is light (1 Jn 1.5), and Christ is also light. It is of Him that the Gospel states: "That was the true light, which gives light to every man coming into the world" (Jn 1.9). Jesus Himself said to the disciples: "I am the light of the world" (Jn 8.12). He spoke of Himself to the people: "While you have the light, believe in the light, that you may become sons of light" (Jn 12.36).

The light of the Son and the light of the Father are **one divine light**. St Philaret explains this thus: "When we look at the sun, we see light: from this light is generated the light visible everywhere beneath; but both the one and the other is one light, indivisible, and of one nature. In like manner, God the Father is the everlasting Light. Of Him is begotten the Son of God, who also is the everlasting Light; but God the Father and God the Son are one and the same everlasting Light, indivisible, and of one divine nature."[xiii]

Jesus—Redeemer and Savior

The Church calls Jesus Christ **Redeemer** and **Savior** because His sufferings and death accomplished our redemption and salvation. The Apostle Peter writes: "You know that you were not redeemed with corruptible things, like silver or gold, from your aimless conduct received by tradition from your fathers, but with the precious blood of Christ, as of a lamb without blemish and without spot. He indeed was foreordained before the foundation of the world, but was manifest in these last times for you" (1 Pet 1.18–20).

The Apostle Paul in his Epistle to the Romans speaks of how Jesus Christ was "delivered up because of our offenses, and was raised because of our justification" (Rom 4.25). And further he writes about the redemptive nature of His death: "For while we were still without strength, in due time Christ died for the ungodly. For scarcely for a righteous man will one die; yet perhaps for a good man someone would even dare to die. But God demonstrates His own love toward us, in that while we were still sinners, Christ died for us. Much more then, having now been justified by His blood, we shall be saved from wrath through Him. For if when we were enemies we were reconciled to God through the death of His Son, much more, having been reconciled, we shall be saved by His life" (Rom 5.6–10).

Thomas' assurance. Icon from the workshop of Dionysius. Russia. 1500.

Theories of Redemption

The coming into the world of God in human flesh is the "great ... mystery of godliness" (1 Tim 3.16). For many centuries theologians have tried to articulate this mystery, and people have attempted to explain something that transcends the human intellect by developing various **theories of redemption**.

Thus, for example, some theologians, relying upon the literal meaning of the word "redemption" ("ransom") have asserted that through His death Christ ransomed the human race from the devil.[xiv] Others have considered this interpretation offensive to God and have justly asked who is this devil that demands such a high price for the salvation of mankind.[xv]

In the fourth century the following concept of redemption was proposed—the human person, as a result of his fall from grace, was in captivity to the devil; in order to redeem him, it was necessary to pay compensation to the devil, a ransom; the man Jesus Christ was offered by way of a ransom; the devil accepted it in exchange for mankind; but under the bait of the human nature of Christ there was concealed the "hook" of His divinity that the devil swallowed, but could not contain: thus God deceived the devil.[xvi] This explanation, elegant and witty, in its time was able to make the notion of the mystery of redemption easier, but it can hardly help the modern-day person to grasp the heart of this mystery.

In the middle ages, thinkers in the Latin west devellopped the theory that the sacrifice of the Son of God on the cross took place because of the need to satisfy God the Father's justice. The essence of this theory was the following: people had angered God so much by their sins, their debt before God was so great, that they could not pay it off by any virtues or merits. In order to satisfy God's justice and appease His anger against mankind, a sacrifice was needed, and this sacrifice was offered by the Son of God.

This explanation of the redemption is not accepted in the Orthodox tradition. The Fathers of the Eastern Church spoke of how Christ offered Himself as Gregory the Theologian expressed the matter: a sacrifice to God the Father, but not because *God* needed this sacrifice, but because *we* needed it: "We needed a God made flesh and made dead, that *we* might live."[xvii] It is we, and not God the Father, that have need of the Son of God's sacrifice on the cross. For our salvation we need precisely this God, and no other: **God who was crucified on the cross**.

The Son of God's death on the cross was the outgrowth of God's love towards us: "For God so loved the world that He gave His Only-begotten Son, that whoever believes in Him should not perish but have everlasting life" (Jn 3.16). These words unveil with the utmost fullness the "great mystery" of the incarnation of God and the Savior's death on the cross. From them it follows that God sacrificed His Son out of love for the whole world, and not for a single nation or group of people.

Salvation

From the same words it follows that salvation and everlasting life are the inheritance only of those who have believed in Christ. Before His Ascension into heaven Jesus said to the disciples: "Go into all the world and proclaim the gospel to every creature. He who believes and is baptized will be saved; but he who does not believe will be condemned" (Mk 16. 15–16). Without faith in Jesus as God and Savior, without accepting Baptism and a life according to His commandments, salvation is impossible.

Lamb of God. Bas-relief of the monastery of Sant Pere de Rodes. Spain. 10th c.

Salvation is the most important term in Christian theology. The incarnation of God, according to the Creed, took place "for our salvation." It was for this goal that the Son of God came down to earth, performed miracles, taught people, suffered, died on the cross, and rose from the dead. The Son of God accomplished our salvation "through His teaching, His life, His death and Resurrection," says St Philaret of Moscow.[xviii]

A human being cannot be saved through his own efforts: this is one of the basic truths of Christian theology. In order for us to be saved and to attain union with God, a Savior is needed. This Savior for the whole human race is Jesus Christ, who suffered and died for us. His **divine grace**[21] saves those who believe in

[21] "**Grace**" in Christian theology means a special divine power that has an effect upon the human person and leads him to salvation.

Jesus saves Peter. Mosaic. Monreale, Italy. 12th c.

Him and live according to His commandments.

In answer to the question of whether Christ suffered and died for all people, St Philaret of Moscow writes: "For His part, [the Lord Jesus Christ] offered Himself as a sacrifice strictly for all, and obtained for all grace and salvation; but this benefits only those of us who, for their parts, of their own free will, have fellowship in His sufferings. … We have fellowship in the sufferings and death of Jesus Christ through a lively and hearty faith, through the sacraments, in which is contained and sealed the virtue of His saving sufferings and death, and, lastly, through the crucifixion of our flesh with its affections and lusts."[xix] To the question of why the sufferings and death of Jesus Christ are saving for us, St Philaret replies: Because "He rose again and so laid the foundation for our like blessed resurrection."[xx]

In Christianity, salvation is understood not simply in the sense that God came to peoples' aid. God is not the one who throws a lifejacket to someone drowning and gazes on sympathetically as the one drowning tries to extricate himself from the water: God plunges Himself into the stormy waters of human life so that the drowning person can cling to Him and be saved.

Christianity says to people: take hold of God, keep a tight hold on Him, do not let Him go—and you will never drown. It is this image of God as someone who is not merely sympathetic at a distance, but who shares all of the trials and afflictions of our life that is revealed to people by the God-man Jesus Christ.

The Sacrifice of Love

One of the Old Testament prototypes of the redemptive sacrifice of the Son of God is the story of the sacrifice of Abraham.[22] In this narrative both Abraham and Isaac are presented as fulfilling the will of God. Yet if Abraham knows this will, then Isaac wholly submits himself to the will of his father in spite of the fact that his father's actions are in stark contradiction to common sense, the rules of common human morality, and the traditional family hierarchy. We hear no protest from the lips of Isaac—only one bewildered question. He silently lies down upon the altar and accepts what is happening as the will of God, which for him is the same as the will of his father.

In what way is this biblical story projected onto the story of the suffering and death of Christ? In the story of the passion, the Son of God stands before us, who from the very beginning knows that He has come in order to be a sacrifice for the "ransom for many" (Mt 20.28; Mk 10.45). He knows that He must fulfill the will of the Father who sent Him (Jn 4.34; 6.38). All of His earthly life is a path towards that hour for which He came into the world (Jn 12.27). But if in the Old Testament story of Abraham, at the last minute the angel stayed his hand from committing the sacrifice of his son, then in the story of the Only-begotten Son of God this does not happen: the sentence of the Father is executed so that the sacrifice offered by His Only-begotten Son is redemptive and saving for all of mankind.

[22] See above, pages 6–8.

The New Revelation about the Human Person and about God

The incarnation of God, the life of Jesus Christ on earth, and His suffering and death became a **new revelation about the human person**. In revealing the divine countenance to mankind, Jesus simultaneously revealed the face of genuine humanity. He showed what the human person can and should be. For Christians, Jesus Christ is the absolute ideal of spiritual and moral perfection.

Christ's suffering and death on the cross became a **new revelation about God**. They revealed the face of God in a way that people had never seen before. A God who sheds His blood for people, who suffers and dies on the cross in terrible agony—this God mankind saw for the first time.

The Christian God is not the God preached by deist philosophers, a God who created the world, established natural laws within it, and then retired to allow the world to develop in accordance with its own laws.[23] Neither is He limited to the image of God revealed in the Old Testament, who actively intervenes in human life, performs miracles and signs, yet who at the same time seems remote and inaccessible, out of reach, incomprehensible and invisible, evoking fear, trembling, and terror. Christianity unveiled the same God in a different manner: He does not look down upon the sufferings of people from the heavenly heights, but rather enters the thick of human sufferings, taking them upon Himself and dying for us.

The Second Coming of Christ

During his lifetime Jesus predicted to His disciples that at the end of history He would come again in glory in order to pronounce the final judgment upon every human being (Mt 25.31–46). The entire life of the early Christian Church was filled with the expectation of the

[23] "Deists" are those philosophers of the eighteenth and nineteenth centuries who expounded such views.

The Second Coming. Detail of an icon. Greece. c. 1700.

second coming of Christ. "Come, Lord Jesus!" (Rev 22.20)—this exultant exclamation, which apparently had a liturgical origin, concludes the last book of the New Testament, the Apocalypse (or Revelation).

For Christians, the second coming of the Savior is not a cause for fear. Christians await with joy the day when "God will wipe away every tear from their eyes; there shall be no more death, nor sorrow, nor crying. There shall be no more pain, for the former things have passed away" (Rev 21.4), when "the last enemy that will be destroyed is death" and God shall "be all in all" (1 Cor 15.26, 28). The second coming of Christ will be the final victory of God over the devil, of good over evil. The spiritual gaze of Christians is set toward this event.

[i] Tertullian, *Apology* 17 (cf. ANF 3:32).

[ii] Augustine, *Confessions* 1.1 (cf. NPNF[1] 1:45).

[iii] Cf. Philaret of Moscow, *Catechism* 11, pp. 446–447.

[iv] Philaret of Moscow, *Catechism* 86, p. 459.

[v] Gregory the Theologian, *Oration* 40.5, in St Gregory of Nazianzus, *Festal Orations*, trans. Nonna Verna Harrison, Popular Patristics Series 36 (Crestwood, NY: St Vladimir's Seminary Press, 2008), 101.

[vi] Philaret of Moscow, *Homily on the Day of the Discovery of the Relics of St Alexis of Moscow*, in *Slova i rechi* [Sermons and speeches], 5 vols (Moscow, 1870s; reprint Moscow: Novospassky Monastery, 2003–2007), 3:436.

[vii] Gregory the Theologian, *Oration* 38.9, PPS 36:66–67.

[viii] John of Damascus, *An Exact Exposition of the Orthodox Faith* 16, in John of Damascus, *On the Orthodox Faith: A New Translation of* An Exact Exposition of the Orthodox Faith, trans. Norman Russell, PPS 62 (Yonkers, NY: St Vladimir's Seminary Press, 2022), 98.

[ix] John of Damascus, *An Exact Exposition of the Orthodox Faith* 43, PPS 62:155–158.

[x] Philaret of Moscow, *Catechism* 155, p. 468.

[xi] Gregory Palamas, *Homily* 34.13, "On the Venerable Transfiguration of our Lord and God and Savior, Jesus Christ," trans. Brian Daly, SJ, *Light on the Mountain: Greek Patristic and Byzantine Homilies on the Transfiguration of the Lord,* PPS 48 (Yonkers, NY: St Vladimir's Seminary Press, 2013), 355–366, at 364.

[xii] Symeon the New Theologian, *Ethical Discourse* 13; St Symeon the New Theologian, *On the Mystical Life: The Ethical Discourses*, vol. 2: *On Virtue and Christian Life*, trans. Alexander Golitzin (Crestwood, NY: St Vladimir's Seminary Press, 1995), 169.

[xiii] Philaret of Moscow, *Catechism* 143, p. 467.

[xiv] See, for example, Origen, *Commentary on the Gospel of Matthew* 12.40, ANF 9:471.

[xv] Gregory the Theologian, *Oration* 45.22, PPS 36:182.

[xvi] Gregory of Nyssa, *Catechetical Discourse* 22–24, in Saint Gregory of Nyssa, *Catechetical Discourse: A Handbook for Catechists*, trans. Ignatius Green, PPS 60 (Yonkers, NY: St Vladimir's Seminary Press, 2019), 110–114.

[xvii] Gregory the Theologian, *Oration* 45.28, PPS 36:189.

[xviii] Philaret of Moscow, *Catechism* 195, p. 474.

[xix] Philaret of Moscow, *Catechism* 209–210, p. 476. The phrase "crucifixion of our flesh with its affections and lusts" comes from St Paul (cf. Gal 5.24). It means the struggle with the passions and sinful desires.

[xx] Philaret of Moscow, *Catechism* 212, p. 477.

Annunciation of the Theotokos. Novgorod school. Russia. 16th c.

4. The Holy Spirit

The Creed states that we believe in "the Holy Spirit, the Lord, the Giver of life, who proceeds from the Father, who together with the Father and the Son is worshiped and gloried, who spoke through the prophets." These words indicate that the Holy Spirit is God, whom Christians worship alongside the Father and the Son.

The Spirit of God in Scripture

There are scattered mentions of the Holy Spirit contained already in the Old Testament. At the creation of the world the Spirit of God "was hovering over the face of the waters" (Gen 1.2). The Spirit of God created man (Job 33.4) and man breathes Him (Job 27.3). The Spirit of God, or the Spirit of the Lord, is "the Spirit of wisdom and understanding, the Spirit of counsel and might, the Spirit of knowledge and of the fear of the Lord" (Is 11.2).

The true revelation of the Holy Spirit, however, is to be found in the New Testament. During His earthly life, Jesus Christ was forever accompanied by the Holy Spirit. Even before His birth the angel appears to Mary and says: "The Holy Spirit will come upon you, and the power of the Most High will overshadow you" (Lk 1.35 [KJV, slightly modified]). Jesus is born of a Virgin and the Holy Spirit. John the Baptist, the forerunner of Jesus Christ, is full of the Holy Spirit from his mother's womb (Lk 1.15). He says that the One who comes after him will baptize "with the Holy Spirit and fire" (Mt 3.11; Mk 1.8; Lk 3.16). At the moment of Jesus' Baptism, the Holy Spirit comes down from heaven in the form of a dove and rests upon Him (Mt 3.16; Mk 1.10; Lk 3.22). Immediately after His Baptism, the Spirit leads Jesus into the wilderness to be tempted by the devil (Mt 4.1; Mk 1.12; Lk 4.1).

The Spirit of God moved over the waters. Detail of the mosaic "Creation of the World." Cathedral of St Mark. Venice, Italy. 13th c.

In His preaching Jesus often speaks of the action of the Holy Spirit. He foretells that His disciples will be persecuted, but exhorts them not to think of what to say beforehand, for it is not they who will speak, but the Holy Spirit (Mt 10.20; Mk 13.11; Lk 12.12). Jesus warns that blasphemy against the Holy Spirit will not be forgiven in this age or the next (Mt 12.32; Mk 3.29; Lk 12.10).

When Jesus was not yet glorified, the Spirit did not rest upon His disciples (Jn 7.39). The death and Resurrection of Christ were the necessary condition for His disciples to receive the Holy Spirit. Christ speaks about this in His farewell discourse with the disciples, one of the main themes of which is the sending of the **Comforter**: "And I will pray the Father, and He shall give you another Comforter, that He may abide with you forever, even the Spirit of truth" (Jn 14.16–17 KJV modified); "When the Comforter has come, whom I send to you from the Father, even the Spirit of truth who proceeds from the Father, He will testify of Me" (Jn 15.26 KJV modified); "When He, the Spirit of truth has come, He will guide you into all truth;

The descent of the Holy Spirit on the apostles. Mosaic. Greece. 12th c.

for He will not speak on His own authority, but whatever He hears He will speak; and He will tell you things to come" (Jn 16.13).

After His Resurrection Jesus appears to the disciples and gives them the Holy Spirit by breathing upon them, saying: "Receive the Holy Spirit. If you forgive the sins of any, they are forgiven them; if you retain the sins of any, they are retained" (Jn 20. 22–23). At the same time, He commands the disciples "not to depart from Jerusalem, but to wait for the Promise of the Father, 'which,' He said, 'you have heard from me; for John truly baptized with water, but you shall be baptized with the Holy Spirit not many days from now.' Therefore, when they had come together, they asked Him, saying, 'Lord, will You at this time restore the kingdom to Israel?' And He said to them, 'It is not for you to know times or seasons which the Father has put in His own authority. But you shall receive power when the Holy Spirit has come upon you; and you shall be witnesses to me in Jerusalem, and in all Judea and Samaria, and to the end of the earth'" (Acts 1.4–8).

The event foretold by Jesus happened on the day of **Pentecost**, when tongues of fire descended upon the apostles and "they were all filled with the Holy Spirit and began to speak with other tongues, as the Spirit gave them utterance." The Apostle Peter said when this happened: "Men of Israel, hear these words: Jesus of Nazareth, a man attested by God to you by miracles, wonders, and signs … Him, being delivered by the determined purpose and foreknowledge of God, you have taken by lawless hands, have crucified, and put to death; whom God raised up, having loosed the pains of death, because it was not possible that He should be held by it. … Being therefore exalted to the right hand of God, and having received from the Father the

promise of the Holy Spirit, He poured out this which you now see and hear. For David did not ascend into the heavens, but he says himself, 'The Lord said to my Lord, "Sit at My right hand, till I make Your enemies Your footstool."' Therefore let all the house of Israel know assuredly that God has made this Jesus, whom you crucified, both Lord and Christ.' Now when they heard this, they were cut to the heart and said to Peter and the rest of the apostles, 'Men and brethren, what shall we do?' Then Peter said to them, 'Repent, and let every one of you be baptized in the name of Jesus Christ for the remission of sins; and you shall receive the gift of the Holy Spirit'" (Acts 2.1–38).

The Action of the Holy Spirit in the Church

The mission of the Christian Church began at Pentecost, and it continues to this day, and in it the Holy Spirit continues to act. It is in this action of the Holy Spirit, which is perceived in the Church as the pledge that Christ's teaching will never be distorted, that His ministry will be continued by His disciples and followers. Christ, in remaining the living and active Head of the Church, guides her through the Holy Spirit. The Holy Spirit is the one whom Jesus left in the Church as "another Comforter": He will be with His disciples forever (Jn 14.16) and will speak not for Himself, but in the name of Christ (Jn 16.13–14).

If the Gospels tell us of Christ's earthly ministry, then the book of the Acts of the Apostles is primarily a witness to the action of the Holy Spirit in the Church that Christ founded. The action of the Holy Spirit upon the faithful in Acts is described using the expressions "filled with the Holy Spirit" (Acts 4.8; 4.31; 9.17; 13.9; 13.52) and "receive the Holy Spirit" (Acts 8.15; 8.17); mention is also made of the descent of the Holy Spirit on those who believed (Acts 8.39; 10.44; 11.15). Baptism was accompanied by the descent of the Holy Spirit: when the Apostle Paul in Ephesus preached to a group of disciples, "they were baptized in the name of the Lord Jesus. And when Paul had laid his hands on them, the Holy Spirit came upon them, and they spoke with tongues and prophesied" (Acts 19.5–6).

The Church believes that all of the holy sacraments are performed through the action of the Holy Spirit. The bread and wine at the Liturgy,[1] in particular, become the Body and Blood of Christ through the action of the Holy Spirit. When the bishop lays hands upon men, they become priests by the grace of the Holy Spirit. And every person who is baptized receives "the seal of the gift of the Holy Spirit" in the sacrament of Chrismation.[2]

The power of the Holy Spirit has been made manifest in the lives of many saints from antiquity up until recent times. The great nineteenth-century Russian saint, Seraphim of Sarov, explained to the merchant Motovilov that the aim of a Christian's life is the acquisition of the Holy Spirit. When Motovilov asked what this meant, he saw how the saint was transformed before his eyes like Christ: his face shone brighter than the sun, and a warmth and sweet-smelling fragrance emanated from him. The saint concluded his conversation with his amazed visitor with the words: "What God requires is true faith in Him and His Only-begotten Son. In return for that, the grace of the Holy Spirit is granted abundantly from on high." [i]

Seraphim of Sarov. Icon. Russia. 20th c.

[1] See pages 228 for the discussion of the Liturgy, the main service of the Christian Church, during which bread and wine become the Body and Blood of Christ.

[2] Baptism and Chrismation will be examined in more detail on pages 97–105.

5. The Trinity

Before His ascension into heaven, Jesus commanded His disciples to baptize people "in the name of the Father and of the Son and of the Holy Spirit" (Mt 28.19). Here for the first time all three persons of the Holy Trinity are named in one concise formula. Yet prior to this, the Father, Son, and Holy Spirit had been revealed to people at the moment when Jesus was baptized by John. Then the voice of the Father was heard and the Holy Spirit came down in the form of a dove upon the Son of God.

Baptism of the Lord. Illuminated manuscript. Byzantium. 10th c.

God Is One but in Three Persons

The teaching that **God is one but exists in three persons** is divinely revealed. At the basis of this teaching are the words of Jesus Christ about His Father and the Holy Spirit, a great many of which are found in the Gospel of John. We also encounter in the Apostle Paul many indications of the three divine persons. One of his epistles concludes with the words: "The grace of the Lord Jesus Christ, and the love of God, and the communion of the Holy Spirit, be with you all" (2 Cor 13.14).

The term "**Trinity**" is not found in the New Testament. It did, however, appear in Christian theology not later than in the second century and became a fundamental part of the theological lexicon of the Christian Church. This term signifies the One who is glorified in three persons.

Holy Trinity. Icon. Andrei Rublev. Russia. 1425.

Belief in the Holy Trinity in no way diminishes monotheism—faith in the one God. The Trinity is **not three Gods, but one God**, while each of the persons of the Trinity is not a part of God, but complete God. Thus, the Father is God, the Son is God, and the Holy Spirit is God. And all three together are the one God.

The source of the Divinity in the Trinity is the Father: from Him the Son is begotten and the Holy Spirit proceeds.[3] Both the **begetting** of the Son and the **procession** of the Spirit are not events that take place in time: they are the personal attributes of the Son and the Spirit that are characteristic of them from all eternity. The Church believes that God always abided in three persons and that this truth was revealed to people by the Lord Jesus Christ.

The three persons of the Trinity abide eternally in a bond of love and union of thought and action. Among them there are no conflicts, contradictions, or disharmony, nor can there be. Of His relationship with the Father, Jesus said: "Most assuredly, I say to you, the Son can do nothing of Himself, but what He sees the Father do; for whatever He does, the Son also does in like manner. For the Father loves the Son, and shows Him all things that He Himself does" (Jn 5.19–20). And of the Holy Spirit, Jesus said: "He will glorify Me, because He will take of what is Mine and declare it to you. All things that the Father has are Mine. Therefore I said that He will take of Mine and declare it to you" (Jn 16.14–15).

The Son of God is "an Advocate with the Father" (1 Jn 2.1) for the entire human race. But the Holy Spirit also "makes intercession for us with groanings which cannot

[3] Jesus Christ taught that the Holy Spirit "proceeds from the Father" (Jn 15.26). In accordance with this teaching, the Creed confesses that the Holy Spirit "proceeds from the Father." In the Latin west in the second millenium the teaching became widespread that the Holy Spirit proceeds "from the Father and the Son." This teaching, known as the *filioque* (from Latin meaning "and from the Son") and given the status of dogma in the Catholic Church, was rejected in the Orthodox East as contradicting the testimony of Scripture.

be uttered"; He "makes intercession for the saints according to the will of God" (Rom 8.26, 27).

Prayer to the Father, the Son, and the Holy Spirit

In prayer the faithful turn to the Father, and to the Son, and to the Holy Spirit separately, and to the three persons of the Trinity together.

An example of prayer to the Father is the Lord's Prayer.[4] Other examples are the prayers read by the priest at the Liturgy, which are addressed mostly to God the Father.

Examples of prayers addressed to Jesus Christ are very numerous. One of them is the "Jesus Prayer," as it is commonly called (or "the Prayer of the Heart"): "Lord Jesus Christ, Son of God, have mercy on me, the sinner." Many prayers said in worship are addressed to Jesus Christ.

An example of prayer addressed to the Holy Spirit is the prayer that many Christians read before the start of any undertaking:

> O heavenly King, the Comforter,
> the Spirit of Truth,
> who art everywhere and fillest all things;
> Treasury of blessings and Giver of life:
> Come and abide in us,
> cleanse us from all impurity,
> and save our souls, O Good One.

An example of prayer to the three persons of the Trinity is the ancient hymn sung at the Liturgy and included in many sequences of prayer: "Holy God, Holy Mighty One, Holy Immortal One, have mercy on us." We believe that

[4] This prayer will be discussed on pages 186–187.

each of the three petitions is addressed to one of the persons of the Holy Trinity: the first to the Father, the second to the Son, and the third to the Holy Spirit. Yet the entire prayer together is addressed to the one and undivided Trinity.

There is yet one more prayer:

> O most Holy Trinity, have mercy upon us;
> Lord, cleanse us from our sins;
> Master, pardon our transgressions;
> Holy One, visit us and heal our infirmities,
> for Thy name's sake.

Here "Lord" refers to the Father, "Master" to the Son, and "Holy One" to the Holy Spirit.

Ship of Salvation. Russia. c. 17th c.

[i] From the conversation of St Seraphim of Sarov with Nikolai Motovilov, recounted in Chapter 7, "The Peace and Warmth of Grace," *Little Russian Philokalia*, vol. 1: *Saint Seraphim of Sarov*, trans. Seraphim Rose (Platina, CA: St Herman of Alaska Brotherhood, 2008), 98–107; the quote is on p. 104.

6. The Church

In the Creed we state that we believe "in one Holy, Catholic, and Apostolic Church."

What is the Church?

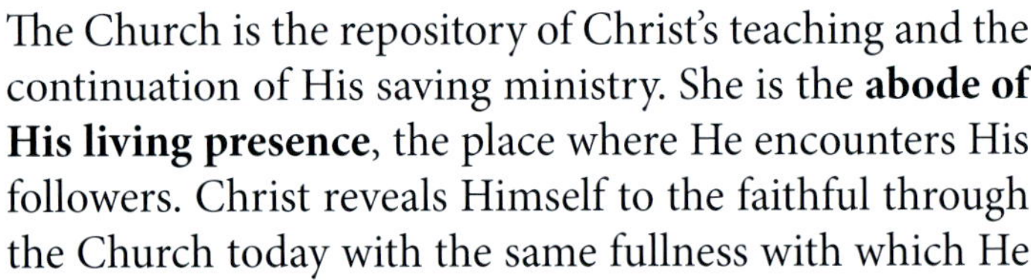

The Church is the repository of Christ's teaching and the continuation of His saving ministry. She is the **abode of His living presence**, the place where He encounters His followers. Christ reveals Himself to the faithful through the Church today with the same fullness with which He revealed Himself to His disciples: His presence in the Church has not diminished; His grace has not become less; His saving power has not dissipated or been lost.

Apostle Peter. Encaustic icon. Saint Catherine's Monastery. Mount Sinai, Egypt. 6th c.

Belief in the Church is one of the basic dogmas of Christianity. It is even said that "there is no Christianity without the Church." Christianity is not just the rational recognition of the value and significance of the person and teaching of Christ. Christianity is primarily membership in the community of His disciples. And this community is the Church.

Christianity cannot be reduced either to a moral teaching, or to theology, or to worship. Nor is it the totality of these things. Christianity is the revelation of the person of the God-man Christ through His Church.

The Foundation of the Church

The Gospel of Matthew narrates how Christ once asked His disciples: "'Who do men say that I, the Son of Man, am?' So they said, 'Some say John the Baptist, some Elijah, and others Jeremiah or one of the prophets.' He said to them, 'But who do you say that I am?' Simon Peter answered, 'You are the Christ, the Son of the living God.' Jesus answered and said to him, 'Blessed are you, Simon Bar-Jonah! For flesh and blood has not revealed this to you, but My Father who is in heaven. And I also say to you that you are Peter, and on this rock I will build My Church, and the gates of Hades shall not prevail against it'" (Mt 16.13–18).

This episode received different interpretations in the Christian East and West. In the West, the role of Peter as the head of the apostolic community and the vicar of Christ on earth, who transmitted his primacy to the bishops of Rome, was emphasized. In the East a different interpretation prevailed: the Church is based on faith in the divinity of Jesus Christ, as confessed in Peter's words. St Peter himself in his epistle insists that the foundation stone of the Church is not Peter, but Christ (1 Pet 2.4).

Why Is the Church Necessary?

The Church is necessary primarily because it **leads people to God** by revealing the heavenly Father to them, uniting them with Christ, and sustaining them with the grace of the Holy Spirit. The Church opens before us the depths and beauty of the Gospels and helps us to embody in our lives the Savior's commandments. Through Baptism, the Eucharist, and the other sacraments, the Church makes us a part of the kingdom of heaven by making it a reality in our lives. Thanks to the Church, this kingdom, like a mustard seed, grows within us and becomes a mighty tree (Mt 13.31–32). Like the leaven in the dough (Mt 13.33), she fills our lives with content and meaning. It is no accident that the Church is called "heaven on earth."

The Church is necessary so that through the grace and power of God **people can be changed for the better**. Many come to the Church spiritually desolate, in despair, and incapable of leading a fully human life. Gradually, by participating in worship, in prayer, by taking Communion and receiving the other sacraments, these people change. The Church helps them to communicate with the living God and to overcome the abyss that divides them from Him. The Church kindles the hearts of people with the fire that is capable of inspiring them to good deeds and creative achievements.

The Church is necessary in order **to change the world**. But no person can change the world without first changing himself. Very often we would like to change the people around us. Often families fall apart because husband and wife try to change each other, instead of working on themselves: one offers remedies to the other on how to be better and as a result the family is destroyed because they cannot agree with each other.

The Church helps people not to think of themselves as individuals who are called to transform others, but as members of a single community in which each, by the action of the Holy Spirit, works on himself and all together help each other to be transformed according to the image and likeness of Christ. Upon entering the Church, the human person enters a powerful current, whose waters begin to transport him to the goal of spiritual perfection. At the same time, the human person does not lose his independence and freedom, but, on the contrary, he acquires new strength to unleash the spiritual and creative potential God has given him.

The Church—the Body of Christ

The Apostle Paul defines the Church as **the body of Christ** (Col 1.24), as a living organism in which each member has a unique function, vocation, and ministry (1 Cor 12.28–30). He states: "For as the body is one and

The Church—the ship of salvation. Contemporary icon.

has many members, but all the members of the body, being many, are one body, so also is Christ. For by one Spirit we were all baptized into one body—whether Jews or Greeks, whether slaves or free—and all have been made to drink into one Spirit. For in fact the body is not one member but many. … Now you are the body of Christ, and members individually" (1 Cor 12.12–14, 27).

The head of the body of the Church is Christ (Eph 4.15). He unites within Himself both the living and those who have departed in the faith. It is in Him that they find the ultimate source of joy and blessedness.

The Two Natures of the Church

The Church was founded on earth, but has a heavenly origin. In the same way that the Founder of the Church, Jesus Christ, has two natures, divine and human, so too the Church has **two dimensions**: earthly and heavenly.

The earthly Church is a "divinely instituted community of men, united by the Orthodox faith, the law of God, the hierarchy, and the sacraments."[i] The heavenly Church includes the spiritual world—the angels, the saints, and all those who have died in the truth faith.

Sometimes the earthly Church is known as the "Church militant" (that is, she is constantly at war with the evil of this world), or the *ecclesia peregrinans* (that is, a Church that is on a journey or pilgrimage), while the heavenly Church is referred to as the "Church triumphant" (that is, as having already attained her goal and having obtained victory over evil).

The Unity of the Church

The Church is one because she was created according to the image of the one God. She is one throughout all of the earth. The unity of the Church throughout the whole world is ensured by the unity of the faith of her members and the unity of the Eucharist in which they all participate.[1]

The Apostle Paul likens the unity of the Church with Christ to the unity between a husband and his wife. He metaphorically describes the Church as a pure virgin betrothed to one husband—Christ (2 Cor 11.2). Christ is the head of the Church and the Savior of the body. He "loved the Church and gave Himself for her, that He might sanctify and cleanse her with the washing of water by the word, that He might present her to Himself

The Eucharist. Mosaic. Church of the Protection of the Theotokos. Moscow, Russia. 21st c.

[1] More will be said of the Eucharist on page 228.

a glorious church, not having spot or wrinkle or any such thing, but that she should be holy and without blemish." The Church submits to Christ as a wife to her husband, while Christ nourishes and sustains her because "we are members of His body" (Eph 5.22–30).

The Sanctity of the Church

The Church is holy according to the image of God who created her and who is holy by nature. The sanctity of the Church is not diminished by the sins of her members. The sanctity of the Church is derived not from the totality of the merits and virtues of her earthly members, but from the sanctity of Jesus Christ, whose body she is.

In being holy by her nature, the Church herself sanctifies all of her members. This sanctification takes place through the Church's sacraments, including Confession and Communion. In the sacrament of Confession we repent of our sins before God and receive forgiveness from Him, which helps us—perhaps not immediately—to free ourselves from our sins. And in the sacrament of Holy Communion we receive within ourselves Christ under the species of bread and wine.

Jesus Christ said to His disciples: "You are the salt of the earth; but if the salt loses its flavor, how shall it be seasoned? It is good then for nothing but to be thrown out and trampled under foot by men. You are the light of the world. A city that is set on a hill cannot be hidden. Nor do they light a lamp and put it under a basket, but on a lampstand, and it gives light to all who are in the house. Let your light so shine before men, so that they may see your good works and glorify your Father in heaven" (Mt 5.13–16).

These words point towards the role that Christians are to play in the world. Like the soul within the body, they are to spiritualize the life of the world. Like salt in food, they are called to make peoples' lives full of content and meaning by protecting human society from vice and destruction brought about by enmity, hatred, conflicts, and vengeance. The presence in the world of the Church—a community of people called to live by loftier moral laws than those proposed by earthly legislation—transforms the world from within, changes it for the better, and raises mankind to a higher level.

Christians are called to holiness and perfection. Jesus says: "Therefore you shall be perfect, just as your Father in heaven is perfect" (Mt 5.48). This call may seem impossible to fulfill because no person is absolutely perfect. And it truly would be impossible to fulfill if there were no Church. She, in being holy and perfect, sanctifies and perfects all of her members. And Christ, as her head, leads every one of her members who so desires to sanctity and perfection. He not only shows the way, but He also leads his followers along this way.

The Catholicity of the Church

The Church is "catholic" (or, in the literal translation from the Greek, "universal"[2]) because she exists throughout the whole world and is open to every human being, regardless of ethnic background and social status. St Cyril of Jerusalem writes: "She is called Catholic because she extends over all the world, from one end of the earth to the other; and because she teaches universally and completely all the doctrines which ought to come to men's knowledge, concerning things both visible and invisible, heavenly and earthly; and because she brings into subjection to godliness the whole race of mankind, governors and governed, learned and unlearned; and because she universally treats and heals the whole class of sins, which

[2] The Greek word *katholikē*, translated as "Catholic," is also used to denote the Western Church that separated from the Eastern Church in 1054. The Eastern Church has always used the adjective "Catholic" to describe herself. After the schism of 1054, the main adjective used for the Eastern Church has been "Orthodox." It was not unusual to find both words in a single name. For example, the Russian Orthodox Church before the 1917 Revolution was officially called the "Russian Orthodox Greek Catholic Eastern Church."

are committed by soul or body, and possesses in herself every form of virtue which is named, both in deeds and words, and in every kind of spiritual gifts."[ii]

The Universal Church consists of local Churches, each of which in its turn is divided into dioceses administered by bishops. The diocese is made up of parishes—church communities administered by priests.

Catholicity is the most important characteristic of the Church. She is Catholic on all levels of her existence—universal, local, diocesan, and parochial. At the universal and local levels, the catholicity of the Church is guaranteed by the unity of the faith of all the episcopate, clergy, and laity.[3] At the local level, the Church is governed by councils of bishops, each of whom at these councils represents not himself personally, but his church community, including the clergy and the people of God.

The Church Hierarchy

To be a member of the Church is to be in union with the church hierarchy: the bishops and priests to whom God has entrusted pastoral care for his flock.

The church hierarchy should not be understood as a power placed above God's inheritance in order to rule over it. The Apostle Peter speaks of this: "I exhort the elders among you to tend the flock of God that is in your charge, exercising the oversight, not under compulsion but willingly, as God would have you do it—not for sordid gain but eagerly. Do not lord it over those in your charge, but be examples to the flock" (1 Pet 5.1–3).

The bishops and priests are members of the body of Christ in the same way as the laity. But they have a special ministry: on behalf of the people they stand before God at the celebration of the Eucharist; they administer

[3] By "clergy" we mean all of those ordained for service in the Church: bishops, priests, and deacons. The laity are those members of the Church who have not been ordained to the clergy or become monks or nuns.

the Church within the boundaries allocated to them and carry out their pastoral care for the souls entrusted to them. This is why the Apostle Paul calls upon the faithful to be obedient to the church hierarchy: "Obey those who rule over you, and be submissive, for they watch out for your souls" (Heb 13.17).[4]

The church hierarchy consists of three degrees: **the bishops, the priests, and the deacons**. The bishops are the direct successors of the apostles, whereas the priests and the deacons are not. Priests receive the right to serve from the bishop, to celebrate the divine offices and the sacraments with his permission and on his behalf. The deacons help the bishops and priests in celebrating the divine offices, but cannot celebrate them by themselves.

The Apostolicity of the Church

St Irenaeus of Lyons (second century) wrote: "It is not necessary to seek the truth among others which it is easy to obtain from the Church; since the apostles, like a rich man [depositing his money] in a bank, lodged in her hands most copiously all things pertaining to the truth: so that every man, whosoever will, can draw from her the water of life."[iii]

The Church is apostolic by virtue of the fact that she carries out the mission of preaching and baptizing that the Lord Jesus Christ commanded His disciples to carry out (Mt 28.19).

Although the Founder of the Universal Church is the Lord Jesus Christ, the founders of the first local Churches were the apostles or their successors. In the first years of the Church's existence the apostles began to

[4] Clergy enjoy authority in the Church, but none of them possesses infallibility: every clergyman as a human being can make mistakes. Within the Church there are certain mechanisms for correcting such mistakes: thus, for example, a bishop can point out a priest's mistakes to him, and if the priest refuses to repent, then he can be punished; a bishop can be punished by the higher ecclesiastical authorities (a council of bishops). Ecclesiastical courts exist to try clergy who are in error.

ordain presbyters[5] and bishops for the governance of the local Churches, which had appeared as a result of the apostolic preaching. This is how apostolic succession in the Church began.

The **apostolic succession** of the hierarchy is a key concept in the Orthodox teaching on the Church: only the Church that possesses an unbroken succession of the hierarchy going back to the apostles is the true Church of Christ. If this succession is absent or has been broken, then the church community cannot be considered to be true, nor its hierarchy legitimate, nor its sacraments valid.

Yet there is nothing automatic or magical in the apostolic succession: the succession of the laying on of hands is not an autonomous line independent of the Church. The bishops and presbyters were ordained by the apostles with the consent of the whole Church, and this consent was no less significant a factor than the event of lawful ordination. The line of apostolic succession is valid only within the Church: outside the Church it loses its validity and meaning.

The Apostle Peter ordains a bishop. Mosaic. Cathedral of St Mark. Venice, Italy. 12th c.

The Church is apostolic also because she retains the apostolic teaching and spreads it throughout the world. No single person has the right to change this teaching formulated by the apostles on the basis of the words of Christ the Savior Himself.

The Church—a Caring Mother

The Church is a **spiritual Mother** for the Christian. The prayer and love of the Church accompany him throughout his earthly journey. When a child is born to a Christian family, he is brought to the church to receive

[5] The Greek word *presbyteros* means "elder." This is what priests were called in the early Church (and to this day in the Greek-speaking Churches).

Hierarchy in the Orthodox Church

Clergy

Servants of the Church who, in the sacrament of ordination receive a special gift of the grace of the Holy Spirit to perform the sacraments and worship, teach people the Christian faith, and manage the affairs of the Church. There are three degrees of the priesthood: bishop, priest, and deacon. In addition, all clergy are divided into monastic and non-monastic clergy; in some traditions, these are referred to as "white" and "black" clergy.

Pentecost, the day of the descent of the Holy Spirit on the Apostles, is called the birthday of the Church

1. Bishop

(Greek: overseer)
highest church rank

Titles of Bishops:

- **Bishop**
- **Archbishop**—a distinguished bishop*
- **Metropolitan**—bishop of the main city, region, or province or most honored bishop
- **Primate**—the chief bishop in the local Orthodox Church; titles used by different primates include patriarch, archbishop, and metropolitan

- A bishop is ordained by a council of bishops (that is, several bishops together) in the sacrament of Holy Orders through a special episcopal consecration.
- In the modern usage observed in churches of the Russian tradition, only a monk can become a bishop.
- The bishop has the right to perform all sacraments and church services.
- As a rule, a bishop is at the head of a diocese, a church district, and cares for all the parish and monastic communities included in his diocese, but he can also perform special church-wide and diocesan obediences without having his own diocese.
- Vicar (Latin: *vicarius*)—a bishop, assistant to another bishop or his vicar.

* In the Greek churches, the order differs slightly, and the titles "archbishop" and "metropolitan" are reversed (the order given above follows the Russian tradition, which the OCA also follows). Likewise for priests and deacons, the honorific titles listed below follow the Russian tradition.

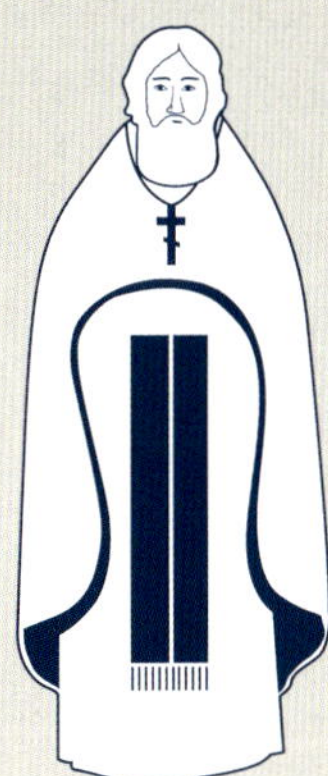

2. Priest

(Greek *presbyteros*, "elder") the second of the sacred ranks

Titles of priests

from the non-monastic clergy

- **Priest**
- **Archpriest**—title usually awarded for distinguished service; may function as a dean
- **Protopresbyter**—a special title, awarded rarely, as a reward for the most worthy and honored priests

from the monastic clergy

- **Hieromonk**
- **Hegumen** (Greek, "leader")—abbot of a monastery
- **Archimandrite** (Greek,"head of a monastery")—in ancient times the abbot of individual famous monasteries, in modern usage an honored hieromonk

3. Deacon

(Greek "minister" or "servant") the lowest sacred rank

Titles of deacons

from the non-monastic clergy

- **Deacon**
- **Protodeacon**—senior deacon
- **Archdeacon**—senior protodeacon

from the monastic clergy

- **Hierodeacon**
- **Archdeacon**—senior hierodeacon

- A deacon is ordained by a bishop in the sacrament of ordination through diaconal ordination.
- The deacon assists the bishop or priest in performing divine services and the sacraments.
- The participation of a deacon in divine services is not mandatory.

Servers

Servants of the Church who do not have the special gift of grace of the sacrament of Priesthood and are assistants to the clergy

- Subdeacon—helps the bishop during hierarchical services.
- Reader—reads and sings during services.
- Altar servers—the most common designation for assistants in worship (young servers may be called "altar boys"); they typically are present in the sanctuary to assist the priest during services. Ringing the church bells may be assigned to altar servers, but in many parishes this task is assigned to people with special training.

Baptism and Chrismation. While still a child, he can participate in the sacrament of Holy Communion, and when he reaches an appropriate age he can go to Confession. The Church sanctifies through her blessing all of the important events in the life of the human person, including Marriage. When he is ill, the priest comes to him to perform the sacrament of Unction for him. When he is dying, the priest comes to him to give him Communion for the last time and Pray for his peaceful departure from this earthly life. When he dies, the Church accompanies him on his last journey and then still remembers him in continuing to pray to God that He grant him blessedness and life everlasting.

Like a caring mother, the Church leads the Christian through earthly life and opens up to him the gates of the kingdom of heaven. It is no accident that in antiquity the principle was formulated that "for those for whom the Church is not mother, God is not their Father."[6] Of course, God cares also for people outside and beyond the Church. But it is in the Church that God interacts with people in a special way, and only in the Church is true union with Him possible. This happens primarily through the Church's sacraments.

Faith and the Church—Orthodoxy

Faith and the Church are closely interlinked. Orthodox worship states that "this is the faith of the apostles, this is the faith of the holy fathers, this is the Orthodox faith."[iv] These words point towards the most important qualities of the true Christian faith, while at the same time highlighting the characteristics of the Church.

The term "**Orthodox,**" particularly, is used in relation to both the faith and to the Church. In Greek it

[6] These words are a paraphrase of the formula from *On the Unity of the Catholic Church* 6, by St Cyprian of Carthage (third century): "He cannot have God as his Father who does not have the Church as his mother." St Cyprian of Carthage, *On the Church: Select Treatises,* trans. Allen Brent, PPS 32 (Crestwood, NY: St Vladimir's Seminary Press, 2006), 157.

His Beatitude Metropolitan Tikhon of All America and Canada, the Primate of the Orthodox Church in America.

comes from the adjective *orthos*, meaning "correct," and the noun *doxa*, which has the double meaning of both "opinion" and "glory." The literal translation of the Greek word *orthodoxia* would be the "correct opinion" or the "correct teaching" (on God). In the Slavic tradition, however, translators have preferred a different rendering of this word, which, translated in turn into English, means "right glorification" (of God). Thus the Slavic tradition emphasizes a mainly liturgical understanding of the faith. To be an Orthodox Christian means not only to have the correct belief about God, but also to worship Him correctly.

The Orthodox Church is the One, Holy, Catholic, and Apostolic Church that was founded by Jesus Christ, which the Creed confesses. She has preserved Christ's teaching pure and undefiled,[7] the teaching of His apostles and the holy Fathers.[8]

[7] The Russian Orthodox Church has made the following statement concerning those communities that have fallen away from unity with the Orthodox Church: "Through the lips of the holy Fathers the Orthodox Church asserts that salvation can be obtained only within the Church of Christ. But, at the same time, those communities which have fallen away from unity with the Orthodox Church have never been viewed as having been deprived of divine grace. The rupture of Church communion inevitably leads to the damaging of a life of grace, but not to its complete disappearance in the communities which have separated. Hence the practice of receiving into the Orthodox Church those who come from non-Orthodox communities not exclusively through the sacrament of Baptism. In spite of the rupture of unity, there remains an incomplete communion which serves as a pledge for the possibility of returning to unity within the Church" (*The Basic Principles of the Relationship of the Russian Orthodox Church to the Non-Orthodox Churches* 1.15).

[8] The holy Fathers are those theologians who formulated the dogmatic teaching of the Church. The most productive period for the formulation of this teaching was the period of the early Church (the first to the third centuries) and the period of the Ecumenical Councils (the fourth to the eighth centuries). The foundations of this teaching were laid in the period of the early Church, while at the seven Ecumenical Councils this teaching was formulated as a counterweight to heresies that had arisen in the meantime.

---

[i] Philaret of Moscow, *Catechism* 252, p. 483.

[ii] Cyril of Jerusalem, *Catechetical Homily* 18.23 (NPNF[2] 7:139–140, lightly edited).

[iii] Irenaeus of Lyons, *Against Heresies* 3.4.1 (ANF 1:416–17).

[iv] Cf. *The Decree of the Holy, Great, Ecumenical Synod, the Second of Nicea* (NPNF[2] 14:549–51, at 551–51).

7. Baptism

The Creed states "I acknowledge one Baptism for the remission of sins."

7.1. Baptism—the Sacrament of the Church

The first thing we need to know about Baptism is that it is not simply a ritual. **Baptism is a sacrament.** In the language of the Church, sacraments are those sacred actions in which God exercises a direct power upon us in granting His saving grace to us.

Baptism is one of the seven sacraments of the Church. Among the other sacraments alongside Baptism are Chrismation, Communion, Repentance, Holy Orders, Matrimony, and Anointing with oil (Unction).[1] But it is Baptism that is the first sacrament, the one with which a Christian's life begins. It is Baptism that opens the doors into the Church and admits one to all the other sacraments; it is what makes one a member of the Church.

Baptism is **spiritual birth**. Jesus spoke about this to Nicodemus in his discourse with him: "'Most assuredly, I say to you, unless one is born again, he cannot see the kingdom of God.' Nicodemus said to Him, 'How can a man be born when he is old? Can he enter a second time into his mother's womb and be born?' Jesus answered, 'Most assuredly, I say to you, unless one is born of water and the Spirit, he cannot enter the kingdom of God. That which is born of the flesh is flesh, and that which is born of the Spirit is spirit'" (Jn 3.3–6).

[1] Chrismation will be spoken of in this chapter, while the other sacraments will be explained in Part 3 (The Church and Divine Worship), Chapters 8 and 9.

Baptism unites the human person with God, bestows upon him the power to withstand the devil and lead a Christian life. Baptism does not spare us from physical sickness, but it does help us to overcome spiritual ailments, which in Christian language are called sins, and which exert a negative influence on the spiritual and bodily composition of the human person. Many illnesses are the direct or indirect result of a sinful way of life. In helping us to be free of sin, the Church enables our healing, thereby strengthening us both in spirit and in body.

The Church believes that in the sacrament of Baptism **all sins are forgiven**. Sins committed after Baptism can be cleansed in the sacrament of Repentance (Confession).

The Baptism of Christ. Icon. Russia. 17th c.

Baptism in the New Testament

Historically, Christian Baptism was preceded by the baptism of John (Mt 3.1–12; Mk 1.4–8; Lk 3.3–17). By its content it was "a baptism of repentance for the remission of sins" (Lk 3.3).

After Jesus was baptized by John, He "and His disciples came into the land of Judea, and there remained with them and baptized" (Jn 3.22). Soon He gave His disciples the right to baptize people (Jn 4.2). As He ascended into heaven, He commanded them to teach all nations and baptize them (Mt 28.19). At Jesus' direct command, the disciples started to preach and receive into the Church through Baptism all those who believed. Baptism was the act that signified entrance into the Church and opened up the way to full participation in church life.

Catechesis

Baptism was always preceded by **catechesis**—the teaching of the truths of the Christian faith. It could be quite short or long, lasting from a few hours or days up to a few weeks, months, or even years. The Book of Acts tells of the eunuch, a man of great authority under the Queen of Ethiopia, who was travelling in a chariot and reading the passage in the book of the prophet Isaiah that spoke of the coming Christ (Is 53.7–8). The Apostle Philip approached the chariot and asked: "Do you understand what you are reading?" The eunuch replied: "How can I, unless someone guides me?" He asked Philip to come up and sit with him. Then Philip "opened his mouth, and beginning at this Scripture, preached Jesus to him." They then approached the water and the eunuch asked: "See, here is water! What hinders me from being baptized?" Philip replied: "If you believe with all your heart, you may." The eunuch said: "I believe that Jesus Christ is the Son of God." These words were a short confession of faith, which was sufficient to be baptized. The apostle baptized

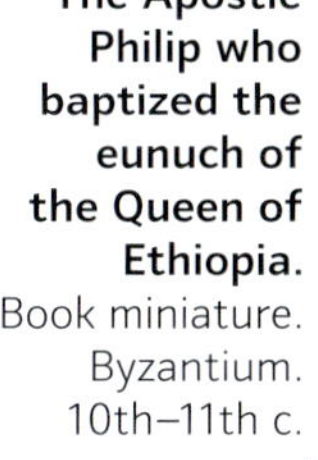

The Apostle Philip who baptized the eunuch of the Queen of Ethiopia. Book miniature. Byzantium. 10th–11th c.

the eunuch, and after the Baptism, the Holy Spirit came upon him (Acts 8.27–39).[i]

In our time also catechesis precedes Baptism. It is very important that a mature person approach Baptism consciously—so that he does not perceive Baptism merely as a ritual in which he can participate, but without understanding its meaning. This is why preparation is essential.

If Baptism is performed for an infant, then of course conscious faith is not required of him. But faith is required from his parents and godparents. The parents ought to be prepared to bring the child up in the Christian faith, while the godparents are there to help them in this.

The Baptism of Infants and Adults

The Baptism of infants is an ancient practice that has existed in the Church since apostolic times. Sometimes one encounters the opinion that Baptism is an act of coercion over the infant: let the child grow up and decide for himself what he believes. This is wrong. The mother breastfeeds the child without ever asking the child about it. And children are sent to school not because they ask for this, but because it is necessary to do so. From earliest infancy we need food, not only in the material sense, but also in the spiritual. Divine grace begins to act upon the child before he can become aware of it. And it is wrong to deprive a child of the divine presence.

It may happen that an adult person does not know whether he is baptized or not: he may think that he was baptized as a child but he is not sure. In this instance he should approach a priest and tell him about this. In such cases Baptism is performed, but as a rule the words "if not already baptized" are added to the baptismal formula.

If someone was baptized in infancy, but then for many years lived without believing and is returning to the Church, then Baptism is not repeated. The Creed states that we "confess *one* Baptism." This emphasizes the unique and unrepeatable nature of Baptism. Even if someone departs from the Church, the grace of Baptism does not leave him, and when he returns to the Church, it renews its effect.

Baptism of Prince Vladimir. Miniature from the Razdivill Chronicle. Russia. 15th c.

Baptism is the **divine seal** that cannot be washed away. At the same time, Baptism may actually lose its power in those people who no longer go to Church, who do not go to Confession and receive Communion, who lead a non-Christian life, and who do not strive to live by the Gospel insofar as this is possible.

In the early Church the sacrament of Baptism was performed as a rule on great feast days, primarily at Pascha, and the pre-Paschal period was the time for preparation. From this ancient practice, Lenten worship has retained the special prayers of Holy Illumination, which at the Liturgy for Holy Saturday is expressed by the change from dark to light-colored priestly vestments.

At present Baptism can be performed on any day by agreement with the local priest. In order to be baptized or to baptize a child, one has to go into a church and speak to a priest or someone else in the leadership of the parish. They can explain what things are necessary, such as a baptismal cross and a white baptismal gown.

The person being baptized (or in the case of an infant one of the parents or a godparent) ought to know the Creed and read it aloud, and understand the meaning of what is being said.

Godparents (Sponsors)

A godparent (godfather or godmother, or sponsor) can be only a person who is a practicing churchgoer—that is, an Orthodox Christian who regularly goes to Confession and receives Holy Communion, and who strives to live according to the Gospel and church teaching. Someone who belongs to another religion or to another Christian confession, even more so a non-Christian, cannot be a godparent. One ought not to choose as a godparent a "non-practicing" Orthodox Christian—that is, someone who only formally belongs to the Orthodox Church.

It is not necessary to have two godparents—it is sufficient to have one (in this instance he or she should be of the same sex as the one being baptized).

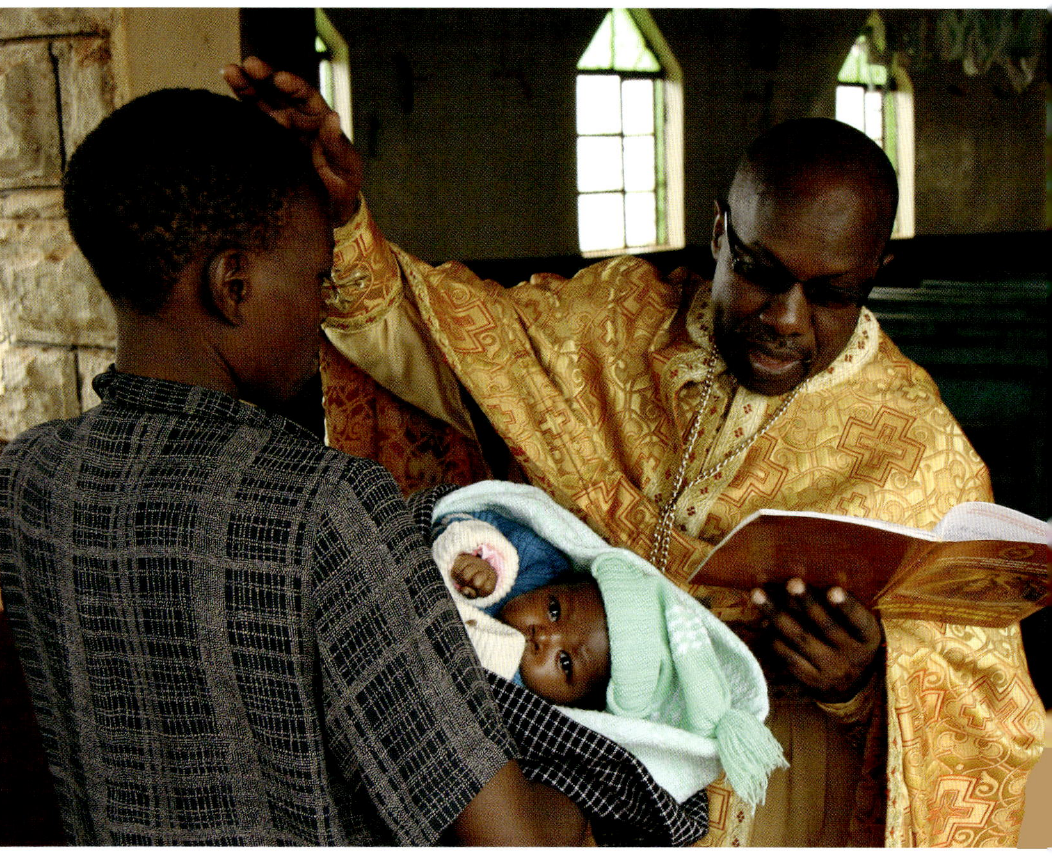

Before Baptism. An Orthodox church in Africa.

Baptism—the Beginning of the Great Journey

We should not be baptized simply because everyone else is, or because our parents oblige us to, or because our friends advise us to do so. It is wrong to baptize a child merely to prevent an illness, or so that he studies well, or so that he listens to his parents. Baptism signifies the entrance of a human being—whether an adult or a child—into the Church. In receiving Baptism, we become members of the Church with all the rights and obligations that follow from this.

Baptism is a special event in a person's life, no less important than his birth into the world. The day of one's Baptism is a joyful and memorable day. This day can be described by the words of the psalm: "This is the day which the Lord has made; let us rejoice and be glad in it" (Ps 117.24).

Yet we ought not to think that receiving Baptism or baptizing a child is a stopping point. On the contrary, it is only from this moment that the journey of a Christian life begins. And this journey is a long one, lasting throughout our whole life. More than that—it does not end with death, but continues into eternity.

7.2. The Service of the Sacrament of Baptism and Chrismation

Following the tradition of the early Church, the contemporary service of Baptism includes two parts—catechesis and Baptism proper. "Catechesis" describes the series of prayers and sacred actions preceding Baptism.[2] Catechesis can be performed separately from Baptism, but in practice it comes immediately before it.

The Beginning of the Office for the Reception of Catechumens

The reception of catechumens begins with a prayer that the person being baptized be filled with faith, hope, and love; when reading this prayer, the priest lays his hands upon the candidate for Baptism. Then a series of exorcisms follows: these are texts addressed not to God, but to the devil. In these exorcisms, the priest commands the devil to leave the candidate for Baptism and to approach him no more. After the exorcisms there are two prayers addressed to God: in them the priest asks God to drive out all impure spirits from the one being baptized, to drive away all actions of the devil, to crush Satan beneath

[2] In this instance "catechesis" is the concluding part of what was meant by "catechumenate" in the early Church: the process of preparation for Baptism.

his feet, to grant him victory over Satan and the other impure spirits, to open the candidate's inner gaze, to illumine him with the light of the Gospel, and to appoint for him a guardian angel, who will deliver him from all influence of the devil.

The priest then breathes cross-wise upon the candidate for Baptism, praying to God: "Expel from him *(her)* every evil and impure spirit which hides and makes its lair in his *(her)* heart." Following Christ's teaching, the heart is the source not only of good but also of evil within a human being (Mk 7.21–22), and therefore before Baptism the heart is to be cleansed by divine grace.

The Renunciation of Satan

Then the priest performs the rite of **the renunciation of Satan**. The priest turns the candidate for Baptism towards the west and asks the question: "Do you renounce Satan, and all his angels,[3] and all his works, and all his service, and all his pride?" To this thrice-repeated question the candidate answers three times: "I do." To the question: "Have you renounced Satan?" he answers three times: "I have." Then the priest calls upon the candidate for Baptism to breathe and spit upon Satan. This ancient rite at times evokes a smile in some people today, but it has deep symbolic meaning: in renouncing Satan, we are laying down a challenge and openly declaring that from that moment onwards we are on the side of God. The Christian life is not leisurely, but a spiritual battle with dark and evil forces. The Apostle Paul states: "Put on the whole armor of God, that you may be able to stand against the wiles of the devil. For we do not wrestle against flesh and blood, but against principalities, against powers, against the rulers of the darkness of this age, against spiritual hosts of wickedness in the heavenly places" (Eph 6.11–12).

When we are baptized and thereby issue a challenge to the devil, at the same time we receive the power of

[3] That is, the fallen angels—the demons (see Mt 25.41).

grace, which enables us to expel further the evil within us and to overcome the temptations that come from the devil. The prayers for the reception of catechumens stress that the devil's power over us is only apparent, illusory: armed with the power of grace, we can now overcome these temptations.

Union with Christ

After the renunciation of Satan, the candidate for Baptism turns to face the east (that is, towards the altar of the church) for the solemn declaration of his **union with Christ**. The priest asks him three times: "Have you united yourself to Christ?" and he answers three times: "I have united myself to Christ." After this the candidate for Baptism (or the godparent on his behalf) reads the Creed aloud. Then the priest calls upon the candidate for Baptism to bow down before God the Father, the Son, and the Holy Spirit, and reads a prayer over him so that God will call him to the sacrament of Baptism proper. The reception of the catechumen ends with this rite.

The Blessing of the Water

Next follows the actual **sacrament of Baptism**. Petitions and prayers are pronounced over the water for it to be sanctified with the power, action, and descent of the Holy Spirit, so that the grace of redemption and the blessing of Jordan may be sent down upon it, so that the purifying operation of the Trinity may come upon it, and so that it may prove effectual in the averting of every snare of enemies, both visible and invisible. Prayers are added for the church community and for the candidate to be baptized: that he may be worthy of the kingdom of God, that he may be a child of light and heir of eternal good things, that he may be a member and partaker of the death and Resurrection of Christ, that he may preserve the baptismal garment and the pledge of the Spirit pure and undefiled at the dread Day of Judgment.

In the prayers at the blessing of the water the priest primarily glorifies God for His majesty and gives thanks to Him for the many blessings He bestows upon the human race, the most important of which was the coming of the God-man into the world. Christ's own Baptism at the hands of John is also recalled. The priest entreats that the grace of the Holy Spirit will come down upon the water and make it "the water of redemption, the water of sanctification, the purification of flesh and spirit, the loosing of bonds, the remission of sins, the illumination of the soul, the laver of regeneration, the renewal of the Spirit, the gift of adoption to sonship,[4] the garment of incorruption, the fountain of life."[ii]

Baptism

Immersion in water is preceded by the rite of anointing with holy oil in the form of a cross on the forehead, ears, breast, hands, and feet of the baptismal candidate. Then the priest immerses him in the water three times with the words: "The servant of God *(name)* is baptized in the name of the Father, amen; and of the Son, amen; and of the Holy Spirit, amen." This is the actual moment of Baptism.

Water fulfills a special role in Baptism: as the symbol of purity and cleansing, it washes the person's body while simultaneously freeing his soul from sins and spiritually renewing him. In the Orthodox Church Baptism is per-

[4] Adoption in God occurs through the sacrament of Baptism (Rom 8.15; Gal 4.6).

Baptism in a river.

formed by full immersion (the Greek verb *baptizō* means "immerse" or "plunge"). In exceptional cases, Baptism is possible by pouring or even by sprinkling water (if, for example, someone is gravely ill, on the verge of dying, or on a life-support machine).[5]

The descent into the water symbolizes death, while the emergence from the water symbolizes resurrection. The Church teaches us that we are born again in Baptism (Jn 3.3–8) in that we have "put off the old man with his deeds, and have put on the new man who is renewed in knowledge according to the image of Him who created him" (Col 3.9–10).

[5] If for whatever reason Baptism was performed by a priest by infusion or sprinkling, it cannot afterwards be "topped up" by another Baptism by immersion since Baptism is performed only once.

Chrismation

Baptism. Mosaic. Cathedral of St Mark. Venice, Italy. 12th c.

In the Orthodox Church the sacrament of **Chrismation** is joined to the sacrament of Baptism. It is performed immediately after the baptismal candidate emerges from the water and is vested in a white robe—the symbol of purity and renewal (at this moment a baptismal cross is traditionally placed around the newly-baptized person's neck).

Chrismation is the sacrament in which we receive "the seal of the gift of the Holy Spirit." When pronouncing these words, the priest anoints the forehead, eyes, ears, nostrils, lips, breast, hands, and feet of the one who has been baptized, with specially consecrated chrism (sometimes called "myrrh") made from sweet-smelling oils. Chrism is prepared under the direct supervision of the primate (the head of a local Church), who distributes it to the dioceses, and each parish receives it from the diocesan bishop. Thus, not only does the chrism blessed and distributed by the primate manifest the gift of the Holy Spirit, it also shows symbolically the link between primate, bishop, priest, and the individual Orthodox Christian.

Anointing is an ancient custom: in the Old Testament the prophets anointed the kings to rule, and through anointing priests were appointed to their ministry. In the New Testament the hereditary Levitical priesthood[6] was abolished, and all Christians came to be seen as "a chosen generation, a royal priesthood, a holy nation, [God's] own special people" (1 Pt 2.9). Accordingly, the ancient rite of anointing was also reinterpreted, and anointing became available to all those who followed Christ "who loved us and washed us from our sins in His own blood, and made us to be kings and priests to His God and Father" (Rev 1.5–6).

6 The Levitical priesthood was the priesthood of the Old Testament. According to its rule, only a man descended from the biblical Levi could become a priest—that is, the priesthood was passed on from father to son.

Chrismation.

In His person Jesus Christ combines the ministry of king and priest. He also grants His followers the power to be kings and priests in the sense that a Christian is called upon to rule over his sinful passions. The Christian sees his life as service to God, returning to God with thanksgiving the gifts that he has received from Him.

The Baptismal Procession and the Reading from Scripture

After Chrismation there follows a procession, in which all the participants in the sacrament—the priest, the newly-baptized, and the godparents—go three times around the baptismal font. This rite has been preserved from the times when people were baptized on the eve of Pascha and they solemnly entered the church building in white garments, where they were greeted by the church community.

Next a text from the Epistle of Paul to the Romans is read: "Do you not know that as many of us as were baptized into Christ Jesus were baptized into His death? Therefore we were buried with Him through baptism into death, that just as Christ was raised from the dead by the glory of the Father, even so we also should walk in newness of life. For if we have been united together in the likeness of His death, certainly we also shall be in the likeness of His resurrection, knowing this, that our old man was crucified with Him, that the body of sin might be done away with, that we should no longer be slaves of sin. For he who has died has been freed from sin. Now if we died with Christ, we believe that we shall also live with Him, knowing that Christ, having been raised from the dead, dies no more. Death no longer has dominion over Him. For the death that He died, He died to sin once for all;

but the life that He lives, He lives to God. Likewise you also, reckon yourselves to be dead indeed to sin, but alive to God in Christ Jesus our Lord" (Rom 6.3–11).

In a way, this reading is a summary of the sacrament of Baptism, while at the same time it reveals its profound meaning. The apostle's words bring to life the symbolism of immersion in the waters of the baptismal font as an image of the Lord's death. Baptism means that the life, death, and Resurrection of Christ become part of a Christian's spiritual experience. At the same time, the apostle emphasizes the moral meaning of Baptism as death to sin and resurrection to a "renewed life."

After the reading of the Epistle there follows a reading from the Gospel, which recounts the commandment that Christ gave to His disciples: to baptize **in the name of the Father, and of the Son, and of the Holy Spirit** (Mt 28. 16–20). This reading testifies that the sacrament of Baptism was established by God. At the same time it also reminds us of Christ's constant presence in the Church: "And lo, I am with you always, even to the end of the age" (Mt 28.20).

The reading of the Gospel is the culmination of the sacrament of Baptism. In modern practice, rites then follow that were performed on the eighth day after Baptism in the early Church: the removal of the myrrh from the body of the newly-baptized candidate and the tonsuring of the hair as a sign of submission to God. The "churching" is also performed: the newly-baptized is led to the "royal doors" of the iconostasis, and he venerates the icons of the Savior and the Theotokos. It is the practice to bring newly-baptized boys into the sanctuary and take them around the altar.

---

[i] The detail of the Spirit's coming upon the eunuch is the reading of the Russian Synodal Translation of the Bible; it is found in the Slavonic lectionary, and in a number of Greek manuscripts, but it is not found in the current Greek lectionary or common English translations. See Bruce Metzger, *A Textual Commentary on the Greek New Testament,* 2nd ed. (Stuttgart: Deutsche Bibelgesellschaft, United Bible Societies, 1971), 316.

[ii] *Baptism*, ed. Paul Lazor (Syosset, NY: Orthodox Church in America, Department of Religious Education, 1972), 51–52.

The angel of the Lord carries the souls of the righteous to heaven. Icon. Russia.

8. The Resurrection of the Dead

The Creed concludes with the words: "I look for the resurrection of the dead and the life of the world to come. Amen."

Belief in an Afterlife

All of the known ancient religious traditions possessed a belief in a **continued existence after the grave**, even though they understand life after death in different ways. Thus, for example, some Eastern religions accept the

The Ladder of Divine Ascent. Fresco from the Sucevița Monastery. Romania. 16th c.

notion that the soul, upon departing the body, can transmigrate into another body, including that of an animal. Christianity rejects this notion, believing that the soul and body are united once in a unique human person. At the moment of death, the soul is separated from the body and begins a different life in another world.

Death—the Transition to Everlasting Life

The problem of the meaning of death has troubled mankind throughout all the ages. Why do we die? Why can we not avoid death? Is immortality possible? Christianity answers these questions thus: **death is the transition to everlasting life**, which for those people who have pleased God will be better than this present life. In the present life, good is intermingled with evil, joys are inevitably accompanied by sorrows. This will not be so in eternity:

there the righteous will contemplate the divine countenance and abide in unceasing joy and peace.

The human person is created for immortality, and he acquires this immortality thanks to his faith in Christ. Death's power is overcome in Christ, and the human person, while dying bodily, continues to live spiritually by passing over to a different place already prepared for him, a world that is more beautiful and perfect. In this world the kingdom of Christ, as the Creed states, "has no end." The fate of people after death, however, is not identical for everyone. The final sentence on the soul of every person will be pronounced at the **Last Judgment**.

Angel rolling up the sky into a scroll. Fresco. Church of St Cyril. Kiev, Ukraine. 12th c.

The Last Judgment and Just Deserts after Death

Not long before his death, Jesus Christ uttered the following words: "When the Son of Man comes in His glory, and all the holy angels with Him, then He will sit on the throne of His glory. All the nations will be gathered before Him, and He will separate them one from another, as a shepherd divides his sheep from the goats. And He will set the sheep on His right hand, but the goats on the left. Then the King will say to those on His right hand,

'Come, you blessed of My Father, inherit the kingdom prepared for you from the foundation of the world: for I was hungry and you gave Me food; I was thirsty and you gave Me drink; I was a stranger and you took Me in; I was naked and you clothed Me; I was sick and you visited Me; I was in prison and you came to Me.' Then the righteous will answer Him, saying, 'Lord, when did we see You hungry and feed You, or thirsty and give You drink? When did we see You a stranger and take You in, or naked and clothe You? Or when did we see You sick, or in prison, and come to You?' And the King will answer and say to them, 'Assuredly, I say to you, inasmuch as you did it to one of the least of these My brethren, you did it to Me.' Then He will also say to those on the left hand, 'Depart from Me, you cursed, into the everlasting fire prepared for the devil and his angels: for I was hungry and you gave Me no food; I was thirsty and you gave Me no drink; I was a stranger and you did not take Me in, naked and you did not clothe Me, sick and in prison and you did not visit Me.' Then they also will answer Him, saying, 'Lord, when did we see You hungry or thirsty or a stranger or naked or sick or in prison, and did not minister to You?' Then He will answer them, saying, 'Assuredly, I say to you, inasmuch as you did not do it to one of the least of these, you did not do it to Me.' And these will go away into everlasting punishment, but the righteous into eternal life" (Mt 25.31–46).

The Last Judgment. Icon. Russia. 15th c.

These words reveal the essence of the Christian concept of reward after death. A person's life in eternity is the continuation of his life on earth: if he loved God here, and strove to fulfill His commandments and do good things, this means that he will abide with God there. If on earth he opposed God and served the devil, then he will be in the power of the devil after death too.

Since God is not the author of evil, neither is He the creator of hell. Hell is created by the actions of the devil, the demons and those people who consciously go against the will of God, who choose the path of evil instead of the path of good. God "**desires all men to be saved** and to come to the knowledge of the truth" (1 Tim 2.4). But not all people desire this. God does not save people forcibly against their will. In going against the will of God, some people create hell for themselves and for those around them—first here on earth, and then this hell continues for them in the life to come.

By His Resurrection Christ vanquished death and opened the gates to everlasting life for all people without exception. If after death not all people go to paradise, then it is because not all people choose the way of God—the way of good. God forces nobody into either paradise or hell. The posthumous fate of the human person is the choice of that very person. At the Last Judgment God will pronounce sentence upon every human being, yet all of us decide our own fate in eternity by our deeds and way of life.

Belief in the Resurrection

Resurrection of Christ. Detail of an icon. Russia. 15th c.

The words "I look for the resurrection of the dead" point towards the Christian teaching that **all people will be raised up**. The Apostle Paul speaks of this resurrection: "For as in Adam all die, so in Christ all shall be made alive. But each one in his own order: Christ the first fruits, afterward those who are Christ's at His coming. Then comes the end, when He delivers the kingdom to God the Father, when He puts an end to all rule and all authority and power. For He must reign till He has put all enemies under His feet. The last enemy that will be destroyed is death" (1 Cor 15.22–26).

The Church believes that the universal resurrection will be bodily: people will be raised in the flesh. Even in the Old Testament the righteous Job said: "I know that my Redeemer lives, and He shall stand at last on the earth; and after my skin is destroyed, this I know, that in my flesh I shall see God" (Job 19.25–26). The book of the prophet Isaiah states: "Your dead shall live, together with my dead body they shall rise. Awake and sing, you who

dwell in dust; for your dew is like the dew of herbs, and the earth shall cast out the dead" (Is 26.19). In the book of the prophet Ezekiel we are presented with an allegorical picture of the universal resurrection: the prophet sees a field where there is a multitude of dead bones; at God's command the bones begin to join one another, grow veins and flesh; finally, God breathes the spirit of life into them and they come to life (Ezek 37.1–11).

What will the bodies of the raised be like—the same as now or will they be different? Christian theology gives no direct answer to this question. It is possible that the external appearance of the body will be changed as the external appearance of the risen Christ changed in such a way that those closest to Him did not immediately recognize Him.

The Victory over Death

Christians ought not to fear death, for they know that **Christ conquered death**. This belief is reflected in the words of the Paschal hymn:

> Christ is risen from the dead,
> trampling down death by death,
> and upon those in the tombs
> bestowing life.

Christ knocks at the door of the heart of every person, yet not all people open the door for Him. To those who respond to His preaching He grants the kingdom of heaven and life with God the Father: "Behold, I stand at the door and knock. If anyone hears My voice and opens the door, I will come in to him and dine with him, and he with Me. To him who overcomes I will grant to sit with Me on My throne, as I also overcame and sat down with My Father on His throne" (Rev 3.20–21).

Amen

The Creed concludes with the word "Amen." This ancient Hebrew word means "truly." It is taken from Old Testament worship and can often be heard in Christian worship. The word "Amen" indicates the Christian's assent to the content of the Creed.

Assignment:

Buy a copy of the New Testament or Bible if you do not already own one, and read the shortest of the four Gospels—the Gospel of Mark. Do not be concerned if you do not understand everything: what you do not grasp the first time will be understood later. The most important thing for the first time you read this text is to grasp the basic thrust of the earthly story of Jesus Christ, listen to the music of His spoken word, and gaze upon His divine countenance. If you are drawn by His image and feel trust towards Him, everything else will come to you, whether immediately or gradually.

Memorial Day Pilgrimage to St Tikhon's Monastery. South Canaan, Pennsylvania.

Christian Morality

The Ten Commandments of the Old Testament

The Beatitudes

The Old Testament Commandments and Christian Morality

Love of God and Love of Neighbor

Sin and Repentance

Family Ethics

The Upbringing of Children

Women in Church

The Christian Life—the Way of Spiritual Struggle

No person in human history has exercised such influence on the spiritual and moral development of human society as Jesus Christ. Although He possesses none of the elements of a social reformer, over the centuries His teaching has become the reason for profound, radical transformations in relationships among people, not only on the level of personal morality, but also on the social level.

Jesus did not call for the abolition of slavery, but thanks to the Christian understanding of the natural equality between people, slavery was finally abolished. He did not call for change in the political regime or reform of the legal code, but thanks to Christianity human society has created legal mechanisms that form the basis of the life of many countries. Jesus was not a fighter for social rights, yet the notion of human rights is based on Christian teaching. This notion has allowed women and children to become full members of society; it has led to the uprooting of inequality in social rights, of discrimination on the grounds of race or nationality, and of many other defects in the social order that were characteristic of the ancient world.

The transformation of society begins with the moral transformation of the human person. The Old Testament commandments were aimed at preserving the spiritual health and integrity of the people of Israel: for this it was possible, when necessary, to sacrifice individuals. The biblical expression is quite typical: "The uncircumcised male who is not circumcised in the flesh of his foreskin, that person shall be cut off from his people; he has broken My covenant" (Gen 17.14). The violators of the divine commandments had to be cut off and removed as a superfluous and dangerous element that was harmful to the people as a whole.

In the New Testament each person is presented as having dignity in the eyes of God. The moral exhortations of Jesus Christ are addressed not to a single nation, but to all of mankind, while at the same time He appeals to each concrete individual. For Christianity there are no unwanted people—that is, those who can be destroyed for the good of others. Each soul is precious and Christ grants even to hardened criminals the chance to repent: "Christ Jesus came into the world to save sinners," the Apostle Paul emphasizes (1 Tim 1.15). On the cross the Lord granted forgiveness to the repentant thief (Lk 23.40–43).

In His teachings Jesus did not aim to give an exhaustive code of moral laws and statutes. It was the Pharisees and the scribes who attempted to create such a code, yet their approach was completely alien to Jesus. His teachings on moral subjects give the basic vector for the spiritual development of the human person, but they are in no way intended to regulate his entire life and his freedom. On the contrary, they return to the human person the inner spiritual freedom that was taken from him when he became enslaved by the passions and sin.

Many moral and social topics are touched upon in the epistles of the Apostle Paul and in the works of the holy Fathers, yet these authors, too, did not attempt to create an exhaustive guide for Christians on moral issues.

In this part of the Catechism we will not look at topics touching upon social morality.[1] We shall examine only a few key principles of personal and family ethics as they are understood in Christianity.

[1] It is possible to find out about the social teaching of Orthodoxy in the document *The Basis of the Social Concept of the Russian Orthodox Church*, which may be found online: old.mospat.ru/en/documents/social-concepts/.

1. The Ten Commandments of the Old Testament

Christian ethics has its pre-history in the Old Testament. The Book of Exodus tells of the **Ten Commandments** that God gave to the people of Israel through Moses. Here they are in abbreviated form:

---

1. I am the Lord your God ... You shall have no other gods before Me.

2. You shall not make for yourself a carved image—any likeness of anything that is in heaven above, or that is on the earth beneath, or that is in the water under the earth. You shall not bow down to them nor serve them; for I, the Lord your God, am a jealous God, visiting the iniquity of the fathers upon the children to the third and the fourth generations of those who hate Me, but showing mercy to thousands, to those who love Me and keep My commandments.

3. You shall not take the name of the Lord your God in vain, for the Lord will not hold him guiltless who takes His name in vain.

4. Remember the Sabbath day, to keep it holy. Six days you shall labor and do all your work. But the seventh day is the Sabbath to the Lord your God; in it you shall do no work: you, nor your son, nor your daughter ...

5. Honor your father and your mother, that your days may be long upon the earth ...

6. You shall not murder.

7. You shall not commit adultery.

8. You shall not steal.

9. You shall not bear false witness against your neighbor.

10. You shall not covet your neighbor's house; you shall not covet your neighbor's wife … or anything that is your neighbor's (Ex 20.2–17).

These Ten Commandments form the basis of Old Testament morality. They have retained their importance for Christianity too, as witnessed by Jesus' conversation with the rich young man, who "came to Him and said, 'Good Teacher, what good thing shall I do that I may have eternal life?' So He said to him, 'Why do you call Me good? No one is good but One, that is, God. But if you want to enter into life, keep the commandments.' So he said to Him, 'Which ones?' Jesus said, 'You shall not murder,' 'You shall not commit adultery,' 'You shall not steal,' 'You shall not bear false witness,' 'Honor your father and your mother,' and, 'You shall love your neighbor as yourself'" (Mt 19.16–19). Of the Ten Commandments, Jesus quotes the sixth, seventh, eighth, ninth, and fifth, adding to them the commandment on love of neighbor.

Moses receives the Commandements. Contemporary icon.

While Jesus highly valued the commandments of the Old Testament, He nonetheless proposed to His followers a loftier way than the mere obligation to observe them. It was the **way of spiritual perfection**, which He showed to the rich young man and upon which the young man did not wish to embark: "If you want to be perfect, go, sell what you have, and give to the poor, and you will have treasure in heaven; and come, follow Me" (Mt 19.21). The way Jesus proposed does not negate the law of Moses, but it leads us significantly further towards the heights of spiritual perfection. Jesus' attitude towards the Mosaic Law is more fully revealed in the Sermon on the Mount. It is a double-sided attitude. On the one hand, He said: "Do not think that I came to destroy the Law or the Prophets. I did not come to destroy but to fulfill. For assuredly, I say to you, till heaven and earth pass away, one jot or one tittle will by no means pass from the law till all is fulfilled" (Mt 5.17–18). On the other hand, it is the Sermon on the Mount, as we shall see later, that testifies that Christ's moral teaching was not a repetition or broadening or direct continuation of Old Testament morality.

The Old Testament is an integral part of the Christian Bible and has retained its importance as a divine revelation granted to mankind at a certain stage of its development. Many Old Testament provisions concerning morality, however, have been reinterpreted and broadened in the Christian tradition, while some have been changed or even abolished.

Thus, for example, the commandment to observe the Sabbath in the way that it is understood in the Old Testament has in reality been abolished in the Christian tradition. At the same time, Saturday remains a special day in the Christian liturgical calendar, when all of the departed are remembered, while Holy Saturday (the day before Pascha) is dedicated to the remembrance of the repose of Jesus Christ in the tomb, the prototype of which was God's rest from His labors on the seventh day of creation. Sunday is the day that Christians dedicate to God in a special way.[i]

The prohibition on killing has retained its meaning in Christianity, extending to those who for whatever reason want to commit suicide. The Church teaches that suicide is a mortal sin.[2] Active voluntary euthanasia—when a person ends his life by means of other people—is also equated with suicide.[3]

The Church has always appealed to peace and considers war an evil, and killing a sin and a crime. At the same time, killing an enemy in wartime is not a sin when defending one's homeland and one's kin.[ii] The Church has always thought highly of the heroic endeavors of soldiers: some warriors have been canonized as saints and are portrayed on icons as carrying arms.[4] The Church describes those warriors who have laid down their life for others on the battlefield using Jesus' words about Himself: "Greater love has no one than this, than to lay down one's life for his friends" (Jn 15.13).

The commandment to honor one's parents is also retained in Christianity (Mt 15.3–6; 19.19; Lk 18.20). Jesus, however, emphasizes that love for Him is higher than any ties of kinship: "He who loves father or mother more

[2] According to *The Basis of the Social Concept of the Russian Orthodox Church*, "a perpetrator of calculated suicide, who 'did it out of human resentment or other incident of faintheartedness' shall not be granted Christian burial or liturgical commemoration (Timothy of Alexandria, Canon 14). If a suicide is committed 'out of mind,' that is, in a fit of a mental disease, church prayer for the perpetrator is allowed after the case is investigated by the ruling bishop. At the same time, it should be remembered that more often than not the blame for a suicide lies also with the people around the perpetrator who proved incapable of effective compassion and mercy. Together with St Paul, the Church calls upon us: "Bear one another's burdens, and so fulfill the law of Christ" (Gal 6.2). [Note also that different local Orthodox Churches may take different approaches to this non-dogmatic issue, some subtly different, some not.—*Ed.*]

[3] On the Church's attitude towards euthanasia see: *The Basis of the Social Concept of the Russian Orthodox Church* 12.8.

[4] For example, those who suffered during the persecutions at the beginning of the fourth century, St George the Victorious and St Demetrius of Thessalonica, the holy martyr John the Warrior who lived at the end of the fourth century, the monks Alexander Peresvet and Andrei Oslybya who perished at the Battle of Kulikovo Field in 1380, and many others.

than Me is not worthy of Me. And he who loves son or daughter more than Me is not worthy of Me" (Mt 10.37). The situation whereby one has to choose between love of Christ and obedience to one's parents arises when the parents go against the Christian faith and try to tear their offspring away from following Christ.

Moses with the Ten Commandments. Philippe de Champagne. France. 17th c.

[i] Cf. Philaret of Moscow, *Catechism* 536–538, p. 527.

[ii] Cf. Philaret of Moscow, *Catechism* 575, p. 535. See also: *The Basis of the Social Concept of the Russian Orthodox Church* 8.2 ("While recognizing war as evil, the Church does not prohibit her children from participating in hostilities if at stake is the security of their neighbors and the restoration of trampled justice"). [St Basil, Canon 13, states "Our Fathers did not consider murders committed in the course of wars to be classifiable as murders at all, on the score, it seems to me, of allowing a pardon to men fighting in defense of sobriety and piety. Perhaps, though, it might be advisable to refuse them communion for three years, on the ground that they are not clean-handed"; *The Rudder*, trans. Denver Cummings (Chicago: Orthodox Christian Educational Society, 1957), 301. This canon was given universal application by the second canon of the Council in Trullo; NPNF[2] 14:361.—*Ed.*]

COVTE ISRAEL
I
SVIS LE SEIGNE
ON DIEV, QVI T'AY
IRE DE LA TERRE
EGIPTE DE LA MAIS
DE SERVITVDE. TV
N'AVRAS POINT D'AV
TRES DIEVX DEVANT
MA FACE. TV NE TE
FERAS POINT D'IDOLE
NI D'IMAGE TAILLEE
NY AVCVNE FIGVRE
POVR LES ADORER.
II
TV NE PRANDRAS PO
LE NOM DV SEIGNE
TON DIEV EN VAIN: CA
LE SEIGNEVR TON DI
EV NE TIENDRA PO
INT POVR INNOCENT
CELVY QVI AVRA PRIS
LE NOM DV SEIGNE
SON DIEV EN VAIN.
III
SOVVIENS-TOY DE
SANCTIFIER LE IOV
DV SABATH.
IV
HONORE TON PERE ET
TA MERE, AFIN QVE T
SOIS HVREVX, ET Q
TV VIVES LOG. TE
SVR LA TERRE.
V
TV NE TVERAS
VI
TV NE COMMETTRAS
PONT FONICATION
VII
TV NE DEROBERA
POINT
VIII
TV NE DIRAS POINT
FAVX TESMOIGNAG
CONTRE TON PROCH
AIN
IX
TV NE DESIRERAS
POINT LA FEMME DE
TON PROCHAIN.
X
TV NE DESIRERAS
POINT SA MAISON. N
SON SERVITEVR. N
SA SERVANTE, NY S
BOEVE NY SON
NY AVTRE
LVY APP

2. The Beatitudes

The Gospels have preserved many of the Savior's teachings. The **Sermon on the Mount** (Mt 5–7) occupies a special place among them. It sets out the moral law according to which Christ calls His followers to live.

We may call the Sermon on the Mount Jesus' self-portrait, since in it He articulated the principles that He embodied in His life and the qualities that He possessed.

The Sermon opens with a series of **Beatitudes**, which contain the essence of Jesus Christ's spiritual and moral teaching:

---

1. Blessed are the poor in spirit, for theirs is the kingdom of heaven.

2. Blessed are those who mourn, for they shall be comforted.

3. Blessed are the meek, for they shall inherit the earth.

4. Blessed are those who hunger and thirst for righteousness, for they shall be filled.

5. Blessed are the merciful, for they shall obtain mercy.

6. Blessed are the pure in heart, for they shall see God.

7. Blessed are the peacemakers, for they shall be called sons of God.

8. Blessed are those who are persecuted for righteousness' sake, for theirs is the kingdom of heaven.

9. Blessed are you when they revile you and persecute you, and say all kinds of evil against for My sake.

Sermon on the Mount. Fresco. Fra Angelico. Italy. 1437–1445.

10. Rejoice and be exceedingly glad, for your reward is great in heaven. (Mt 5.3–12)

This text would at first appear to refute the generally accepted notions of what happiness is. People believe that happiness depends upon material prosperity, on success in their professional activities, on the well-being of their family, on the absence of problems, difficulties, afflictions, and sorrows. Jesus teaches that true happiness (blessedness) in no way depends on external factors: it is our inner inheritance, acquired through personal qualities.

The first in this list of qualities is spiritual poverty, which means **humility**—a special inner spiritual condition that comes from the remembrance of God and the feeling of His presence. Humility is not a synonym for passivity or the state of being humiliated. The Christian is called upon to take up an active position in life and to accomplish good deeds. He is not, however, to claim these good deeds as a result of his merits, recalling that all that he has on the spiritual and material level comes from God. Humility is the opposite of pride (excessive self-reliance and a sense of superiority towards others), which places a barrier between God and the human person and brings a disharmony into our relationships with other people.

The beatitude concerning those who **mourn** shows that the Christian is to endure afflictions with patience, should never fear misfortunes and trials, and should not seek only joys and pleasures in life. In trials we are to see the hand of God and find solace in sensing His presence. The Christian weeps not from being offended or from anger, not from despondency or despair, but from an awareness of his own sins (the tears of repentance), or from joy at being close to God (the tears of loving-tenderness).

Meekness is a quality that, if attained, enables us to find inner peace of soul. Jesus says: "Come to Me, all you who labor and are heavy laden, and I will give you rest. Take My yoke upon you, and learn from me; for I am gentle and lowly in heart, and you will find rest for your souls. For My yoke is easy, and My burden is light" (Mt 11.28–30). In being the exemplar of meekness, the Savior exhorted His disciples to follow Him. And the Apostle Peter appeals to women in his epistle: "Do not let your adornment be merely outward—arranging the hair, wearing gold, or putting on fine apparel—rather let it be the hidden person of the heart, with the incorruptible beauty of a gentle and quiet spirit" (1 Pet 3.3–4). Meekness is a sign of inner beauty that befits both men and women alike.

Christ commands us to hunger and thirst after **righteousness**—that is, we are always, and in all things, to seek out that which is right and just. In the Old Testament righteousness is often presented as one of the qualities of God: He is a "righteous God" (Ps 7.9 NKJV). Human righteousness is a reflection of this divine righteousness. God's righteousness transcends time and has an eternal nature, but it is reflected in the commandments that God gave to us who live in time. Those who "hunger and thirst after righteousness" are those who ardently strive to fulfill the divine commandments, those who seek God with all their heart, the Fount of all righteousness, those who can use their power and position to put an end to iniquity and support those who have been unjustly treated.

The Christian is to be **merciful**, becoming like the Lord in this manner, who is "compassionate and merciful" (Ps 102.8). Mercy ought to be manifested not only within the disposition of one's heart, but also in concrete deeds of kindness—the very same deeds Christ tells us will be required at the Last Judgment: to feed the hungry, give drink to the thirsty, take in the stranger, clothe the naked, visit the sick and those in prison (Mt 25.35–36). The Apostle James, too, speaks of how faith ought to manifest itself in good deeds: "For as the body without the spirit is dead, so faith without works is dead also" (Jas 2.26).

Purity of heart opens up for the human person the way towards a vision of God, who is invisible in His nature, yet reveals Himself to the humble, the meek, and the pure in heart. Purity of heart cannot be acquired merely through one's own efforts; God's help is needed: "Create in me a clean heart, O God, and renew a right

"I was hungry and you fed Me, I was naked and you clothed Me ..." Book miniature. Byzantium. 13th c.

spirit within me" (Ps 50.10). God awaits from us repentance and contrition of the heart: "A sacrifice to God is a broken spirit; a broken and humbled heart God will not despise" (Ps 50.17).

The disciple of Christ is called upon to be a **peacemaker**—that is, to bring peace to those around him. For this he must have an inner peace and unshakeable steadfastness of spirit. St Seraphim of Sarov said: "Acquire the spirit of peace and thousands around you shall be saved." The peacemaker is the one who, while having an inward peace, does not respond to evil with evil. If a conflict flares up anywhere, he makes every effort to quell it.

Christ warns His disciples that they should be prepared for **persecutions**. Throughout the ages persecutions of varying intensity have rained down upon the Church: so it was in the first centuries of her existence, when all of the punitive might of the Roman empire was aimed at her destruction, and so it was in the Soviet Union in the twentieth century, when the Church was subjected to the most ferocious repression.

Holy Martyrs Cyrus and John. Book miniature. Byzantium. 12th c.

But even in times of peace and prosperity to be a Christian means to be ready to lay down a challenge to "this world" with its distorted and inverted notions of happiness, morality, good, and evil. The Beatitudes, which begin the Sermon on the Mount, demonstrate that Christian morality coincides with so-called common human morality in only a few aspects. Common human morality is aimed solely at guaranteeing the peaceful coexistence of subjects who are inwardly hostile towards each other. Christian morality, however, directs the strivings of the human being towards a holiness and spiritual perfection capable of uniting people in the indissoluble bonds of brotherly love in "the knowledge of the mystery of God, both of the Father and of Christ" (Col 2.2).

3. The Old Testament Commandments and Christian Morality

In the Sermon on the Mount Christ raises the moral bar significantly higher than the level towards which Old Testament ethics was orientated. Nevertheless, the moral law that Christ conveys in the Sermon on the Mount essentially complements (and in some instances corrects) the Mosaic Law as set out in the Old Testament.

Killing and Anger

Jesus says to His disciples: "You have heard that it was said to those of old, 'You shall not murder, and 'whoever murders will be in danger of the judgment.' But I say to you that whoever is angry with his brother without a cause shall be in danger of the judgment. And whoever says to his brother. 'Raca!' shall be in danger of the council. But whoever says, 'You fool,' shall be in danger of hell fire" (Mt 5.21–22).

If the Old Testament forbade killing as the most extreme expression of human anger, enmity, and hatred, then Jesus points towards the cause that can lead to murder. We are to **root out anger** in our hearts and refrain from directing hurtful words at our neighbor so that conflicts do not have a tragic outcome; we are to quell conflict in the very place where it is generated: in our own heart.

Oaths and Falsehood

Jesus speaks out against oaths and falsehood: "Again you have heard that it was said to those of old, 'You shall not swear falsely, but shall perform your oaths to the Lord.'

But I say to you, do not swear at all: neither by heaven, for it is God's throne; nor by the earth, for it is His footstool; nor by Jerusalem, for it is the city of the great King. Nor shall you swear by your head, because you cannot make one hair white or black. But let your 'Yes' be 'Yes,' and your 'No,' 'No.' For whatever is more than these is from the evil one" (Mt 5.33–37). The evil one in the New Testament is called the devil—the source of all evil and sin. The devil is also the father of lies (Jn 8.44). In this world the devil's lies go against God's truth: the person who embarks upon the path of falsehood thereby serves the devil.

Non-Resistance to Evil by Force

A most important principle of Christian ethics is formulated in the following words: "You have heard that it was said, 'An eye for an eye and a tooth for a tooth.' But I tell you not to resist an evil person. But whoever slaps you on your right cheek, turn the other to him also. If anyone wants to sue you and take away your tunic, let him have your cloak also. And whoever compels you to go one mile, go with him two. Give to him who asks you, and from him who wants to borrow from you do not turn away" (Mt 5.38–42).

Here Jesus speaks out against the use of retribution, which lies at the basis of many moral systems. This principle was important in order to avert disproportionate vengeance in the socio-cultural milieu described in the time of the Old Testament. But Christ advances a new principle: **do not respond to evil with evil.**

Why does Jesus command us not to respond to evil with evil? Because evil is healed not by evil, but by good: we can uproot evil only through the aid of good. When there is a conflict between two people, moral victory is obtained, from the Christian perspective, not by the one who takes revenge on his offender, but by the one who prevents the conflict from escalating by making compromises, including the sacrifice of his own interests. On the social level this person may look defeated, but his personal victory over evil has greater meaning for him than his own interests, which may have been infringed upon.

The principle of **non-resistance to evil by force** ought not to be perceived as passivity before the evil that acts in the world. The Christian is to fight evil within himself and resist evil within the family, within society, and within his country. He is called to come to the side of the humiliated and oppressed, to defend his homeland when it is in danger, and to protect the Church from desecration.

Love of Enemies

Yet one more very important principle of Christian ethics is expressed in the Savior's following words: "You have heard that it was said, 'You shall love your neighbor and hate your enemy.' But I say to you, **love your enemies**, bless those who curse you, do good to those who hate you, and pray for those who spitefully use you and persecute you, that you may be sons of your Father in heaven; for He makes His sun rise on the evil and on the good, and sends rain on the just and on the unjust. For if you love those who love you, what reward have you? Do not even the tax collectors do the same? And if you greet your brethren only, what do you do more than others? Do not even the tax collectors do so?" (Mt 5.43–47).

In the context in which it was uttered, Jesus' call had a socio-political dimension: to renounce the idea of other peoples as enemies, of gentiles and foreigners as enemies of God, which for the Jews meant nothing other than losing the very earth under their feet, to be deprived of one of the most important parts of their identity, to lose their motivation for national self-determination.

In this commandment Jesus is primarily attempting to widen the framework of His listeners' thinking by compelling them to see that His teaching has a universal character. Jesus does not juxtapose love of enemies to love of neighbor: He widens the notion of "neighbor" to include enemies. The basic thought of His teaching may be conveyed in the following way: our attitude towards another person should never depend upon his attitude towards us; love should not be only mutual; good should not be only in response to something good. In manifesting love and accomplishing good, the Christian is called upon to take up a *pro*-active, and not a *re*-active, position: he should not merely react to the feelings and actions of others, but become a source of love and good.

Jesus Himself manifests precisely this way of acting. Thousands of people flocked towards Him, and He communicated with them, healed their illnesses, listened to their needs, showed them love and kindness without expecting either love or gratitude or reward in return. No single category of people was denied His attention and love, including the publicans and immoral women. Even the Pharisees and scribes were not left without His concern: harsh and irreconcilable towards Pharisaism in denouncing its uglier manifestations, Jesus did not refuse to speak to the Pharisees, to answer their questions, to visit their homes and sit with them at the same table. Concerning the commandment to pray for those who offend and persecute us, He fulfilled it literally when He prayed on the cross for those who had crucified Him (Lk 23.34).

Healing a demon-possessed youth. Fresco. Serbia. 14th c.

The commandment to love one's enemies may be called the essence of all Christian morality; like the focus of a camera, it reflects all of Christ's commandments. It is the commandment to love one's enemies that most significantly of all renews the Old Testament notion of love, of morality, of those criteria upon which our relationship with our neighbor ought to be built. This commandment lays the foundation of the new world, which can be realized in full measure only within the community of Christ's disciples—the Church.

Love is an inward feeling that has not so much a rational as an emotional foundation. For this reason, it is very difficult for us to compel ourselves to love another, to force ourselves to love our enemies, even if, on the intellectual level, we know that this is what we must do. Love of enemies is attained not simply through self-control, it cannot be the result of our decision to relate to our neighbor in one way and not in another. It is true that the acquisition of love for our enemies demands that we work upon ourselves, but this working upon ourselves is not enough. We need also a favorable environment in which we can develop this quality. This environment is the Church.

The moral principles expressed by Christ act primarily within the Church, which is the community of His disciples. Yet the Christian cannot be a Christian only within an environment of people like him: he is to embody Christian moral principles within his life, including in the milieu of people who do not share these principles.

The teaching on love of one's enemies ought not to be seen as a call to refuse to defend the homeland or defend the truth. St Philaret of Moscow wrote: "Avoid the enemies of God, defeat the enemies of the Fatherland, and love your personal enemies."[i]

---

[i] Philaret of Moscow, *Homily on the 19th Sunday after Pentecost* (delivered at some point between 1806 and 1808), in *Slova i rechi*, 1:285–289, at 289.

4. Love of God and Love of Neighbor

The Two Main Commandments

Jesus saw the heart of the Old Testament law in the two commandments that He quoted when He spoke with the scribes, who had asked Him the question: "Teacher, which is the great commandment in the law?" Jesus said to him, "'**You shall love the Lord your God** with all your heart, with all your soul, and with all your mind.' This is the first and great commandment. And the second is like it: '**You shall love your neighbor as yourself.**' On these two commandments hang all the Law and the Prophets" (Mt 22.35–40).

Both of the commandments are taken from the Old Testament (Deut 6.5 and Lev 19.18); in the Christian perspective however, they acquire a new content. In the Old Testament the word "neighbor" was understood to mean a fellow member of the same nation or ethnic group, a son of the same people. In quoting the commandment, Jesus significantly broadens its meaning, taking the word "neighbor" to mean every person, regardless of his ethnic or religious affiliation.

The evangelist Mark records the reaction of Jesus' interlocutor: "So the scribe said to Him, 'Well said, Teacher. You have spoken the truth, for there is one God, and there is no other but He. And to love Him with all the heart, with all the understanding, with all the soul, and with all the strength, and to love one's neighbor as oneself, is more than all the whole burnt offerings and sacrifices.' Now when Jesus saw that he answered wisely, He said to him, 'You are not far from the kingdom of God'" (Mk 12.32–34).

It is not by chance that Jesus' interlocutor refers to the cult of sacrifice. This cult formed in ancient Israel at a time when religious life was primarily seen in juridical terms. Sin was believed to be a crime before God that required atonement: the sacrifice served as this atonement.

Jesus brought a new religion to replace the cult of sacrifices, a religion based on different assumptions: He proposed building up the relationship with God not out of a sense of duty or fear, but by basing it on love and fidelity. Love of God, which embraces all of a person's nature, including the heart, soul, and intellect, is to find its expression not in sacrifices, but in love of neighbor. He speaks of love and kindness, not of sacrifices and religious rites, as the fundamental criteria according to which at the Last Judgment God will separate sinners from the righteous, the sheep from the goats (Mt 25.31–46).

The scribe asks Jesus about only one—the greatest—commandment, yet Jesus in His reply adds a second. This demonstrates that for Him love of God and love of neighbor comprise a single two-sided commandment: one type of love cannot be thought of without the other. Love of God finds its expression and natural continuation in love of neighbor. The Apostle John the Theologian reminds us of this in the following words: "If someone says, 'I love God,' and hates his brother, he is a liar; for he who does not love his brother whom he has seen, how can he love God whom he has not seen? And this commandment we have from Him: that he who loves God must love his brother also" (1 Jn 4.20–21).

The Christian Understanding of Love

The Old Testament gave the commandment to love one's neighbor "as oneself" and it was this that was the culmination of Old Testament ethics. Since the scribe's question exclusively concerned the Law of Moses, Jesus indicated this commandment as one of its two spiritual and moral heights. Proceeding from the notion that every person loves himself and wishes to do good, in the Sermon on the Mount Jesus formulated a rule summing up the Old Testament principle of relating to one's neighbors: "Therefore, whatever you want men to do to you, do also to them, for this is the law and the prophets" (Mt 7.12).

In Jesus' teaching, however, another voice resounds, a different tone can be heard from that in which the moral precepts of the Law of Moses were expressed. And ultimately Jesus calls upon us to love our neighbor not *as* ourselves, but *more* than ourselves. He calls us to be capable of surrendering our life for our neighbor (Jn 15.13). To sacrifice our own life for the sake of another is the goal towards which Christian love aspires.

Love is the fundamental concept of Christian theology and Christian ethics. Christianity is often called the religion of love, if we bear in mind that the teaching on love is at the core of its meaning and values. The Apostle John states: "God is love. In this the love of God was manifested toward us, that God sent His Only-begotten Son into the world, that we might live through Him" (1 Jn 4.8–9). Through His sufferings and death, "having loved His own who were in the world, He loved them to the end" (Jn 13.1). And at the Last Supper He left the commandment to His disciples to love one another as a "new commandment" (Jn 13.34).

What is new in it? The idea that Christ calls upon His disciples to love one another not with a customary love based on mutual regard, but with a sacrificial love, which does not expect love in response. His words refer not to a love that is defined by lover and beloved belonging to a single people. It is not the natural love that exists between people held together by blood ties or the bonds of friendship. Jesus is referring to a qualitatively different love—the one that embraces all of the aforementioned types of love and transcends them in having a supernatural origin. The source of this love is not human sentiments or emotions: its source can only be God Himself.

The Christian teaching on love is realized in full measure only in the Church and it is the Church that is the place where Christians are called to learn love from Christ Himself. Yet the love towards which they are called ought to extend not only to the other members of the Church. It should embrace all people without exception, including our own personal enemies. The Christian ought not to divide people into friends and enemies, into his own and those alien to him. For him, all people are his own, neighbors, and kinsmen. And he is called to love each one, regardless of whether this love is reciprocated or not.

5. Sin and Repentance

Sin

In Christian moral teaching the concept of **sin** plays an important role. The word "sin" does not mean a criminal act or any other violation of human laws. Sin is any falling away by the human person from the moral law as established by God, from the goal for which God had appointed him.[1]

Sin separates a human being from God and leads to spiritual death. The Apostle James says that "each one is tempted when he is drawn away by his own desires and enticed by it. Then, when desire has conceived, it gives birth to sin; and sin, when it is full-grown, brings forth death" (Jas 1.14–15).

People's sins are many and varied and cannot be exhaustively categorized. In early Christian literature there was the notion that there were eight basic sins that emerged from the sinful passions: gluttony, fornication, avarice, wrath, sloth, despondency, vanity, and pride.[i] In the Western tradition there arose the teaching that sins could be divided into mortal sins—that is, more serious, and non-mortal sins—that is, venial. Sometimes sins are divided into three categories: against God, against one's neighbor, and against oneself.

Sins are voluntary and involuntary. A voluntary sin is committed by a person consciously—when he understands that a particular act goes against God's law and yet nevertheless commits it. Sins that are committed by a person in spite of his desire or his will are called involuntary.

Christ says that "whoever commits sin is a slave of sin" (Jn 8.34). Sin enslaves people, making them dependent on their sinful habits and inclinations, on "the lust of the

[1] The Greek word *hamartia*, translated in English as "sin," literally means "missing the mark." It originally was used for an archer whose arrow flew past the target.

A fight. Adriaen van Ostade. Netherlands. 1637.

flesh, the lust of the eyes, and the pride of life" (1 Jn 2.16).

In modern medical terminology, the term "dependency" denotes a person's insistent need for something: we speak of drug and alcohol dependency, dependency upon computer games, and so on. Some forms of dependency are linked to psychiatric disorders; yet very often a person's deep-rooted sinful habits are at the basis of dependency. Thus, for example, alcoholism and drug addiction are sinful from the viewpoint of the Church, since they may lead to a complete breakdown of the personality.[2]

Various forms of dependency are often interlinked: freedom from one form of dependency by purely mechanical means can lead a person towards other forms of dependency. It is in the same way that sins are interconnected, and one sin often leads to another. Thus, for example, the Apostle Paul emphasizes the link between excessive use of alcohol and fornication (Eph 5.18). St Cyprian of Carthage (third century) writes: "If avarice is prostrated, lust springs up. If lust is overcome, ambition takes its place. If ambition is despised, anger exasperates, pride puffs up, wine-bibbing entices, envy breaks concord, jealousy cuts friendship."[ii]

Sins are impossible to overcome solely by willpower or by autosuggestion. In our struggle against sin we must not rely solely upon ourselves: we should call upon God's help and find strength in our faith and Scripture. The Apostle Paul says: "Stand therefore, having girded your waist with truth, having put on the breastplate of righteousness, and having shod your feet with the preparation of the gospel

[2] For the Church's position on alcoholism and drug addiction, see: *The Basis of the Social Concept of the Russian Orthodox Church* 11.6.

of peace; above all, taking the shield of faith with which you will be able to quench all the fiery darts of the wicked one. And take the helmet of salvation, and the sword of the Spirit, which is the word of God" (Eph 6.14–17).

Christianity views sin as a sickness. As a spiritual sickness, sin often has bodily sicknesses as a direct result. Spiritual health, accordingly, affects the entire spiritual-bodily composition of the human person. The Lord Jesus Christ indicated this when He healed the man suffering from palsy and He said to him: "Son, be of good cheer; your sins are forgiven you" (Mt 9.2). To another man suffering from paralysis, whom He had healed, Jesus said: "See, you have been made well! Sin no more, lest a worse thing come upon you" (Jn 5.14).

Repentance

The Church does not accuse a human being of sin, but helps him to become aware of his sins and to heal them. The medicine for sin is **repentance**.

There are no sins that cannot be healed by repentance. Jesus Christ states: "Every sin and blasphemy will be forgiven men, but the blasphemy against the Spirit will not be forgiven" (Mt 12.31). Blasphemy against the Holy Spirit is here usually taken to mean stubborn resistance to God's will, conflict with God, the unwillingness to repent of one's sins and correct oneself.

Repentance is not identical to remorse. Remorse or regret over a particular sin may not bring the required fruits. Judas, who betrayed the Savior for thirty pieces of silver, showed remorse and returned the money to the high priests and elders, saying: "I have sinned by betraying innocent blood" (Mt 27.3–4). He did not truly repent, however, nor did he return to the community of Christ's disciples, but committed suicide, a grave sin that only exacerbated his guilt. The Apostle Peter, by contrast, who had denied Christ, wept bitterly over this denial (Mt 26.69–75), confessed his love for Jesus, and proved

Peter's denial. Duccio di Buoninsegna. Italy. 13th c.

it through the feats of his subsequent life and martyr's death (Jn 21.15–19).

Repentance is not limited to stating the fact of a sinful act and showing regret for it. Repentance is an entire spiritual system, which includes daily self-analysis, contrition for sins committed and sinful thoughts that have been permitted, striving, in as far as possible, to correct the evil that has been done, and constant work upon oneself with the goal of spiritual correction. To repent is to transform one's way of thinking and way of life,[3] to replace sinful deeds with their opposite, to accept the Christian system

[3] The Greek word *metanoia,* which is often translated "repentance," literally means the "transformation of the mind," the "transformation of one's way of thinking."

of moral values, to fulfill God's commandments, to strive unceasingly towards the good not only in our actions, but also in our thoughts and feelings.

The Apostle Paul exhorted Christians: "Put off, concerning your former conduct, the old man which grows corrupt according to the deceitful lusts, and be renewed in the spirit of your mind, and ... put on the new man which was created according to God, in true righteousness and holiness" (Eph 4.22–24). Inward spiritual renewal through repentance leads to our complete moral rebirth.

The God Who Forgives Sins

Repentance returns us to God, who loves every person and waits until he turns away from his sinful lifestyle and returns to Him. In the Old Testament God says: "I have no pleasure in the death of the wicked, but that the wicked turn from his way and live" (Ezek 33.11).

In the New Testament the parable of the prodigal son, uttered by Jesus on the way to Jerusalem, is devoted to the subject of repentance: "A certain man had two sons. And the younger of them said to his father, 'Father, give me the portion of goods that falls to me.' So he divided to them his livelihood. And not many days after, the younger son gathered all together, journeyed to a far country, and there wasted his possessions with prodigal living. But when he had spent all, there arose a severe famine in that land, and he began to be in want. Then he went and joined himself to a citizen of that country, and he sent him into his fields to feed swine. And he would gladly have filled his stomach with the pods that the swine ate, and no one gave him anything. But when he came to himself, he said, 'How many of my father's hired servants have bread enough and to spare, and I perish with hunger! I will arise and go to my father, and will say to him, "Father, I have sinned against heaven and before you, and I am no longer worthy to be called your son. Make me like one of your hired servants."' And he arose and came to his father. But when he was still a great way off, his father saw him and had compassion, and ran and fell on his neck and kissed him. And the son said to him, 'Father, I have sinned against heaven and in your sight, and am no longer worthy to be called your son.' But the father said to his servants, 'Bring out the best robe and put it on him, and put a ring on his hand and sandals on his feet. And bring the fatted calf here and kill it, and let us eat and be merry; for this my son was dead and is alive again; he was lost and is found.' And they began to be merry. Now his older son was in the field. And as he came and drew near to the house, he heard music and dancing. So he called one of the servants and asked what these things meant. And he said to him, 'Your brother has come, and because he has received him safe and sound, your father has killed the fatted calf.' But he was angry and would not go in. Therefore his father came out and pleaded with him. So he answered and said to his father, 'Lo, these many years I have been serving you; I never transgressed your commandment at any time; and

Prodigal son (Traveler). Hieronymus Bosch. Netherlands. 1510.

yet you never gave me a young goat, that I might make merry with my friends. But as soon as this son of yours came, who has devoured your livelihood with harlots, you killed the fatted calf for him.' And he said to him, 'Son, you are always with me, and all that I have is yours. It was right that we should make merry and be glad, for your brother was dead and is alive again, and was lost and is found'" (Lk 15.11–32).

Return of the Prodigal Son. Rembrandt Harmenszoon van Rijn. Sketch. Dutch. 17 c.

In this parable, repentance is shown to be a gradual process beginning with the prodigal son's coming to a state of self-awareness, recalling his father, and deciding to return to him. He then goes from words to deeds. The main actor of the parable, however, is not the son, but the father, who symbolizes God. When a person returns to God and repents, God does not condemn him, but receives him with outstretched arms.

The parable shows that repentance is always an encounter between the human person and God. The father in the parable does not simply wait patiently until the son draws near to him: when he sees him, he runs out to greet him. We do not hear a single word of condemnation or reproach from the lips of the father.

The Lord Jesus Christ says of Himself: "I did not come to judge the world, but to save the world" (Jn 12.47). Jesus said to the woman caught in adultery: "Woman, where are those accusers of yours? Has no one condemned you? ... Neither do I condemn you. Go and sin no more" (Jn 8.10–11). When the Pharisee expected Jesus to condemn the sinful woman who had wiped His feet with precious myrrh, instead of condemning her, Jesus said: "Your sins are forgiven. ... Your faith has saved you. Go in peace" (Lk 7.48, 50). Of those who repented as a result of the preaching of John the Baptist, Jesus said, turning to the Pharisees: "Assuredly, I say to you that tax collectors and harlots enter the kingdom of God before you. For John came to you in the way of righteousness, and you did not believe him; but tax collectors and harlots believed him; and when you saw it, you did not afterward relent and believe him" (Mt 21.31–32).

It Is Never too Late to Repent

It is never too late to repent, and even the most hardened criminal can at the end of his life repent and receive forgiveness from God. This is demonstrated by the example of the wise thief, who was crucified alongside Christ and who became aware of the sinfulness of his former way of life. He turned to Jesus, saying: "Lord, remember me when You come into Your kingdom." To this Jesus replied: "Assuredly, I say to you, today you will be with Me in Paradise" (Lk 23.42–43).

At the same time, repentance should never be put off till a later time, because death may come to any person suddenly. In response to the question of the Galileans who had been killed on Pilate's orders, Jesus said: "Do you suppose that these Galileans were worse sinners than all other Galileans, because they suffered such things? I tell you, no; but unless you repent you will all likewise perish" (Lk 13.1–3).

A person's fate in eternity depends upon how he lived his life on earth, how he built up his relationship with God. Unlike human laws, according to which punishment automatically follows after the crime, a different law operates with God: God frees us from punishment for sins if we sincerely repent of them, turn away from the path of evil, and embark upon the way of good.

---

[i] Cf. John Cassian, *On the Eight Vices*, in *The Philokalia, The Complete Text*, compiled by St Nikodimos of the Holy Mountain and St Makarios of Corinth, trans. G. E. H. Palmer, Philip Sherrard, and Kallistos Ware, vol. 1 (London and Boston: Faber and Faber, 1979), 74–93, at 74.

[ii] Cyprian of Carthage, *On Mortality* (ANF 3:470).

6. Family Ethics

Christ's Teaching on Marriage and Divorce

In the Sermon on the Mount Christ states: "You have heard that it was said to those of old, 'You shall not commit adultery.' But I say to you that whoever looks at a woman to lust for her has already committed adultery with her in his heart. If your right eye causes you to sin, pluck it out and cast it from you; for it is more profitable for you that one of your members perish, than for your whole body to be cast into hell. And if your right hand causes you to sin, cut it off and cast it from you; for it is more profitable for you that one of your members perish, than for your whole body to be cast into hell. Furthermore it has been said, 'Whoever divorces his wife, let him give her a certificate of divorce.' But I say to you that whoever divorces his wife for any reason except sexual immorality causes her to commit adultery; and whoever marries a woman who is divorced commits adultery" (Mt 5.27–32).

Sts Joachim and Anna. Icon. Russia. 15th c.

Here the Savior points first towards the causes that can lead to sins of the flesh and the breakdown of marital fidelity: these causes are rooted in a man's heart, in his evil gaze directed at looking at other men's wives. Second, here the Lord comes across as a principled **opponent of divorce**, permitting divorce only in one instance—

when either husband or wife has violated the principle of marital fidelity.

Once the Pharisees approached Christ with the question: "Is it lawful for a man to divorce his wife for just any reason?" He answered by referring to the biblical story of the creation of the human person: "Have you not read that He who made them at the beginning 'made them male and female?'" And again He quoted Scripture: "For this reason a man shall leave his father and mother and be joined to his wife, and the two shall become one flesh (Gen 2.24). ... Therefore what God has joined together, let not man separate." The Pharisees did not give in, but continued to ask: "Why then did Moses command to give a certificate of divorce and to put her away?" (Deut 24.1). Jesus answered: "Moses, because of the hardness of your hearts, permitted you to divorce your wives, but from the beginning it was not so. And I say to you, whoever divorces his wife, except for sexual immorality, and marries another, commits adultery" (Mt 19.3–9).

This approach seemed too harsh even to the Savior's disciples (Mt 19.10). However, the Church has preserved Christ's teaching on marriage in the form in which He gave this teaching. In her canon law the Church relies upon the notion of the **unique nature and indissolubility of the marriage union**. Divorce is permitted only for the reason indicated by the Savior, as well as for other reasons that would make the continuation of the married state for one or both of the spouses impossible.[1]

[1] *In The Basis of the Social Concept of the Russian Orthodox Church* (10.3) among the reasons for divorce, apart from adultery and one of the spouses entering a new marriage, other grounds are mentioned: the rejection of the Orthodox faith by one of the spouses, unnatural vices, the inability to cohabit that had appeared before marriage or as a result of self-harm, infection with leprosy or syphilis, a lengthy unknown absence, a criminal conviction with the removal of all rights, an incurable mental illness, the intentional abandonment of one of the spouses by the other, infection with AIDS, medically attested chronic alcoholism or drug addiction, or the wife having an abortion without the consent of her husband.

The wedding ceremony.

Second and third marriages are permitted only in the instance of the death of one of the spouses or in other special circumstances foreseen by ecclesiastical rules.[2] However, for the clergy a second marriage is impossible under any circumstances.

The Family—the "Little" Church

In the Christian tradition the **family** is viewed as a "little Church." This notion is founded upon the teaching of the Apostle Paul, who called Christian families of his time

[2] *The Basis of the Social Concept of the Russian Orthodox Church* (10.3) stresses that "divorce as the last resort can be sought only if spouses committed actions defined by the Church as causes for divorce." Nevertheless, "if a divorce is an accomplished fact, especially when spouses live separately, the restoration of the family is considered impossible and a church divorce may be given if the pastor deigns to concede the request. The Church does not at all approve of a second marriage. Nevertheless, according to canon law, after a legitimate church divorce, a second marriage is allowed to the innocent spouse. To those whose first marriage was dissolved through their own fault a second marriage is allowed only after repentance and penance imposed in accordance with the canons. According to the rules of St Basil the Great, in exceptional cases where a third marriage is allowed, the duration of the penance shall be prolonged." The penance is a type of punishment fixed by the Church authorities in each concrete case.

a "domestic church" (Rom 16.5; 1 Cor 16.19; Col 4.15). Within the family circle, Christians of all generations are called to embody in practice the ideal of love that they have been taught in the Church and through the reading of Scripture. Husband and wife are called to build their family life on the firm foundation of the moral teachings of the Gospel.

The Christian marital union is a union "in the Lord." The Apostle Paul writes: "Nevertheless neither is the man without the woman, neither the woman without the man, in the Lord. For as the woman is of the man, even so is the man also by the woman; but all things of God" (1 Cor 11.11–12).

Children are a special gift of God for every family. The Psalter speaks of this: "Lo, sons are the heritage of the Lord, the fruit of the womb a reward" (Ps 126.3). The Savior reminds us of the joys of having children: "A woman when she is in labor, has sorrow, because her hour has come: but as soon as she has given birth to the child, she no longer remembers the anguish, for joy that a human being has been born into the world" (Jn 16.21).

In insisting upon the absolute worth of every human life, Christian ethics categorically forbids abortion by equating it with murder. The right to be born is the inalienable right of every human being. The denial of this right to a human being, whoever he may be, is a grave sin

in the eyes of the Church, and for such a denial an answer before God must be given.[3] The use of those contraceptives that induce abortion is also considered a grave sin.[4]

Orthodox tradition recognizes as a marriage only a **union between a man and a woman**, a union that is founded upon mutual love and that has as one of its main goals the birth of children and their upbringing. "Alternative" forms of cohabitation, which have become widespread in modern society, cannot be considered a marriage and do not receive the Church's blessing.

7. The Upbringing of Children

In the ancient world children were not viewed as fully-fledged members of society. Christianity fundamentally changed this attitude towards children. Modern notions of the dignity and rights of children, which have become an integral part of civilized society, have their roots in a Christian understanding.

Christ and Children

Jesus Christ taught that children should be treated with special care and attention: "Take heed that you do not

[3] For the Church's position on abortion, see: *The Basis of the Social Concept of the Russian Orthodox Church* 12.2.

[4] *The Basis of the Social Concept of the Russian Orthodox Church* (12.3) states: "Some contraceptives have an abortive effect, interrupting artificially the life of the embryo in the very first stages of life. Therefore, the same judgments are applicable to the use of them as to abortion. But other means, which do not involve interrupting an already conceived life, cannot be equated with abortion in the least. In defining their attitude to the non-abortive contraceptives, Christian spouses should remember that human reproduction is one of the principal purposes of the divinely established marital union. The deliberate refusal of childbirth on egoistic grounds devalues marriage and is a definite sin."

Entry of the Lord to Jerusalem. Children meet the Savior. Fresco and its fragment. Serbia. 14th c.

despise one of these little ones; for I say to you that in heaven their angels always see the face of My Father who is in heaven" (Mt 18.10).

The Gospels also describe this episode in the life of the Savior: "Then they brought little children to Him, that He might touch them; but the disciples rebuked those who brought them. But when Jesus saw it, He was greatly displeased and said to them, 'Let the little children come to Me, and do not forbid them; for of such is the kingdom of God. Assuredly, I say to you, whoever does not receive the kingdom of God as a little child will by no means enter it.' And He took them up in His arms, laid His hands on them, and blessed them" (Mk 10.13–16).

There is another scene that is no less characteristic: "At that time the disciples came to Jesus, saying, 'Who then is greatest in the kingdom of heaven?' Then Jesus called a little child to Him, set him in the midst of them, and said, 'Assuredly, I say to you, unless you are converted and become as little children, you will by no means enter the kingdom of heaven. Therefore whoever humbles himself as this little child is the greatest in the kingdom of heaven. Whoever receives one little child like this in My name receives Me. But whoever causes one of these little ones who believe in Me to sin, it would be better for him if a millstone were hung around his neck, and he were drowned in the depth of the sea. Woe to the world because of offenses! For offenses must come, but woe to that man by whom the offense comes!'" (Mt 18.1–7).

By these words the Lord indicates that the criteria for evaluating a particular person in the kingdom of heaven are the opposite of those criteria by which we value people on earth. A child is used as an example: he corresponds to the ideal in the Sermon on the Mount more than an adult. The Christian is called upon to trust God the Father in the same way that children trust their parents.

The Savior also reminds us of the responsibility of adults for the upbringing of children. The abuse of children is a grave sin. Temptations "must come," not because this is the will of God, but because in a world where good and evil are intertwined, temptations, like weeds, grow in the same field as the wheat (Mt 13.24–30). However, the one who sows temptation bears personal responsibility for it, which is greatly exacerbated if the object of sinful or abusive actions, as well as the various forms of propagating sin, are children.

The Christian Upbringing of Children

The **upbringing of children** in the Christian tradition is founded upon the belief that children, no less than adults, need God's grace. And the spiritual development of the child is no less important than his physical growth. That is why from earliest childhood Christian parents make their children a part of church life.

After Communion.

After a child has been baptized, the next thing that should be done is give him Communion. Unlike certain other Christian denominations, where it is believed that only children who have reached a conscious age can take Communion, the Orthodox Church admits infants to Communion in the belief that saving grace has an effect upon them in spite of the fact that they cannot rationally comprehend what is going on around them. After the first Communion the child should be taken to Communion regularly—preferably no less often than every Sunday—so that Communion does not become a rare event for him.[1]

[1] Infants who regularly take Communion react positively to the atmosphere in church and to the sacrament itself. By contrast, infants who are brought infrequently to Communion often perceive it with stress. It is very important that the atmosphere in the church and of worship should not frighten children but, on the contrary, should be welcoming and habitual.

As the child grows closer to a conscious age the basics of the Orthodox faith ought to be explained to him using the simplest of examples. From earliest infancy the child ought to know that God exists in heaven and sees him and hears him, and, most importantly, loves him. From earliest infancy the child ought to recognize in icons the face of Jesus Christ, the Mother of God, the most venerated saints, and to understand who they are. The child ought to read [or at least hear] the Gospel—even in a simplified version—from the earliest age, so that the words of the Savior become deeply embedded in his consciousness. It is also useful to read the *Lives* of the saints and other Christian literature.

Children who are brought up in the faith and who view the Church as their spiritual home receive a powerful vaccination against unbelief and vice for their entire lives. Of course, even the most exemplary Christian upbringing cannot give a full guarantee that when the child reaches maturity, he will not leave the Church. Nevertheless, even in such cases the sound foundations of faith that have been laid down in childhood survive in the depths of a person's soul right up to the moment when he, like the prodigal son from the Gospel parable (Lk 15.11–24), recalls his heavenly Father and desires to return to Him.

The upbringing of children in the Christian family ought to be founded upon **love** and not on compulsion. A child should be taught to choose good and reject evil freely and independently. A common error is the attempt to impose upon children an image of God as someone who punishes them for disobedience to their parents and for other acts. It is far more important to teach a child to love God, Christ, and the Church. And in order to attain this goal, it is essential that all methods of educating the child in the family be built upon love. It is love—not only love founded upon kinship, but also spiritual love founded upon love of God—that unites all members of the family into one "domestic church."

The epistles of the Apostle Paul contain simple advice concerning family life and the relationship between parents and children: "Children, obey your parents in all things, for this well pleasing to the Lord" (Col 3.20); "Children, obey your parents in the Lord, for this is right. 'Honor your father and mother,' which is the first commandment with promise: 'that it may be well with you and you may live long on the earth.' And you, fathers, do not provoke your children to wrath, but bring them up in the training and admonition of the Lord" (Eph 6.1–4).

This advice reflects the methods of childrearing that existed in various nations for many years, but which at present are disputed in those societies that place freedom and the child's independence above all external factors. Religion is often perceived exclusively as one of the means of imposing a particular worldview or particular moral precepts upon the child. Some dispute the Church's right to educate children, believing that it violates their freedom.

The Christian Understanding of Freedom

Freedom, however, is one of the key concepts of Christianity. "For you, brethren, have been called to liberty," says the Apostle Paul, but he immediately adds: "Only do not use liberty as an opportunity for the flesh" (Gal 5.13). Christianity understands freedom not as something detached from moral norms but, on the contrary, as being rooted in the knowledge of truth. Christ said to His disciples: "And you shall know the truth, and the truth shall make you free" (Jn 8.32). The knowledge of truth and communion with God and the Church do not violate a child's freedom. On the contrary, they bestow upon him the spiritual freedom that will help him, as a young child and in adolescence, to withstand corrupting external influences and to preserve an inner strength that will help him keep to the path of good.

8. Women in the Church

In many aspects, Christian moral teaching has been distinguished by its radical novelty in relation to both Old Testament ethics and to the morals spread throughout the ancient world in general. An obvious examples of this is the **attitude of Christianity towards women**.

There is the widely-held view that the Church diminishes the role of women in society and in the family and insists upon preserving a vanished patriarchal way of life. Such accusations against the Church are unjust.

It is precisely within the Christian tradition that women from the very outset have played a role that has made them the equal of men. The Apostle Paul stated: "As many of you as were baptized into Christ put on Christ. There is neither Jew nor Greek, there is neither slave nor free, there is neither male nor female; for you are all one in Christ Jesus" (Gal 3.27–28).

Christ and Women

Alongside the male disciples, there were female disciples who followed Jesus and who were known by name: "Now

Saints Anastasia, Barbara, Euphemia, Marina, Thekla, Christina. Icon. Mount Athos, Greece. 17th c.

Conversation of Christ with the Samaritan woman. Fresco. Catacombs of Pretextata on Via Latina. Italy. 4th c.

it came to pass, afterward, that He went through every city and village, preaching and bringing the glad tidings of the kingdom of God. And the twelve were with him, and certain women who had been healed of evil spirits and infirmities—Mary called Magdalene, out of whom had come seven demons, and Joanna the wife of Chuza, Herod's steward, and Susanna, and many others who provided for Him from their substance" (Lk 8.1–3).

Women are accorded a significant place in the Gospel narratives. We see Jesus conversing with the Samaritan woman (Jn 4.7–26), with Martha and Mary (Lk 10.38–43), with the sinful woman (Lk 7.48), with the woman caught in adultery (Jn 8.10–11), with the woman with an issue of blood (Mt 9.20–22), with the Canaanite woman (Mt 15.25–28), with Mary Magdalene (Jn 20.14–17), and other women (Mt 28.9–10).

The images of women who followed Christ play an important role in all four evangelists' narratives of the sufferings and death of Christ and His Resurrection. Unlike the male disciples, who "forsook Him and fled" (Mt 26.56) when Jesus was arrested, the women continued to follow Him. They stood at the foot of the cross (Mt 27.55; Mk 15.40–41), early in the morning on the first day of the week

Resurrection of Christ ("Do not touch me"). Fresco. Giotto. Italy. 1303–1306.

they came to His tomb in order to anoint His body with sweet-smelling spices, and they were the first to see Him risen from the dead (Mt 28.1–10; Mk 16.9–11; Lk 24.1–10; Jn 20.1–18). It was from these women that the male disciples heard that Christ had risen.

After Christ's Resurrection, the eleven apostles "all continued with one accord in prayer and supplication, with the women and Mary the mother of Jesus, and with His brothers" (Acts 1.14). The death and Resurrection of Christ united those who followed Him during His earthly life into a single community (Acts 1.16). This community was made up of the apostles, Jesus' blood relatives, including His Mother, and the same women who ministered to Him in Galilee.

All of Christ's apostles were men, yet there have been women throughout the Church's history who have been glorified as "Equal-to-the-Apostles" (for example, St Mary Magdalene, St Nina the Enlightener of Georgia, and St Olga of Kiev). Throughout the centuries the apostolic succession of the hierarchy has been transmitted through the male line, and the priesthood is a male ministry. Yet this in no way diminishes the role of women. The issue touches upon not unequal rights but different vocations.

Women's Ministry in the Church

The Apostle Paul notes that "there are diversities of gifts, but the same Spirit. There are differences of ministries, but the same Lord. And there are diversities of activities, but it is the same God who works all in all. But the manifestation of the Spirit is given to each one for the profit of all." And further he expands on the theme that not all people in the Church have identical ministries, but that "God has appointed these in the Church: first apostles, second prophets, third teachers, after that miracles, then gifts of healings, helps, administrations, varieties of tongues. Are all apostles? Are all prophets? Are all teachers? Are all workers of miracles? Do all have gifts of healings? Do all speak with tongues? Do all interpret?" (1 Cor 12.4–7, 28–30).

Women's ministry occupies a special place in the various vocations in the life of the body of the Church. A woman cannot be a bishop or a priest, but she can be the abbess of a convent, she can direct a church choir, she can be a professor of theology, and she can occupy other important positions, including that of church administration.

Yaroslavl Icon of the Mother of God. Russia. 15th–16th c.

Motherhood—A Woman's Unique Vocation

In the same way, according to the Church's teaching, men and women do not enjoy different rights in the family, but they are called to **different vocations**. Only women are said to be "saved in childbearing" (1 Tim 2.15). Bearing and raising children is a woman's unique vocation. The man, of course, takes part in this; a special responsibility, however, is placed upon the woman in this regard. Only a woman can be a mother, and this vocation in the family cannot by be substituted with something else, whereas the father has his own irreplaceable calling.

The Church's attitude towards women can be judged by how highly she regards the Mother of God. The Most Holy Mother of God is the Mother of both Christ and of the Church. It is in her person that the Church glorifies motherhood—the inalienable dignity and privilege of a woman.

The image of the Mother with the Infant in her arms with His cheek tenderly resting upon her cheek is the ideal that the Orthodox Church proposes to every Christian woman. This image, which is present in all Orthodox churches in an endless variety of forms, has a great spiritual attraction and moral force. And while the Church lives, she will always remind women of their main calling in their earthly lives—**to be a mother and to bring up children**.[1]

[1] In the Old Testament childlessness was viewed as a "reproach among people" (Lk 1.25): childless couples were looked upon as sinners to whom God had not granted descendants, as a punishment for their sins. Christianity does not view childlessness as a punishment from God, and the physical incapability of one or other of the spouses to have children cannot be used as grounds for divorce. The Church encourages childless couples to adopt children.

9. The Christian Life—the Way of Spiritual Endeavor

In the Sermon on the Mount the Savior teaches His disciples: "Do not lay up for yourselves treasures on earth, where moth and rust destroy and where thieves break in and steal; but lay up for yourselves treasures in heaven, where neither moth nor rust destroys and where thieves do not break in and steal. For where your treasure is, there your heart will be also" (Mt 6.19–21). Jesus hereby teaches us to be attached neither to material goods, nor to social status, nor to other earthly good things, but to seek always the kingdom of heaven.

The Savior states: "No one can serve two masters; for either he will hate the one and love the other, or else he will be loyal to the one and despise the other. You cannot serve God and mammon" (Mt 6.24). In pursuing earthly good things, the feverish search for wealth becomes incompatible with service to God. First place in the hierarchy of values must be taken by God; all other good things can come afterwards.

In encouraging His disciples not to immerse themselves in earthly cares, Jesus reminds them of Divine Providence: "Look at the birds of the air, for they neither sow nor reap nor gather into barns; yet your heavenly Father feeds them. Are you not of more value than they? Which of you by worrying can add one cubit to his stature? So why do you worry about clothing? Consider the lilies of the field, how they grow: they neither toil nor spin; and yet I say to you that even Solomon in all his glory was not arrayed like one of these. Now if God so clothes the grass of the field, which today is, and tomorrow is thrown into the oven, will He not much more clothe you, O you of little faith? Therefore do not worry, saying, 'What shall we eat?' or 'What shall we drink?' or 'What shall we wear?' For after all these things the Gentiles seek. For your heavenly Father knows that you need all these things. But seek first the kingdom of God and His righteousness, and all these things shall be added to you" (Mt 6.26–33).

By saying this, the Savior does not forbid us from working or providing for ourselves or for our children—He is warning us about becoming enslaved to work and turning labor into a goal in itself. In Christianity, there is no ideal vision of a human person who dedicates all his health and well-being to earthly labor, but who has nothing left for the realm of the spirit. Christianity gives us a picture of a different ideal: the person who lives on earth, but who is not engulfed by the varied and many cares of earthly affairs, and who seeks the "kingdom of God, and His righteousness," who is mindful of our heavenly Father, and who places his hope not so much upon his own efforts, as upon divine providence.

Jesus teaches us: "Enter through the narrow gate; for wide is the gate and broad is the way that leads to destruction, and there are many who go in by it. Because narrow is the gate and difficult is the way which leads to life, and there are few who find it" (Mt 7.13–14). He also says: "If your hand or foot causes you to sin, cut it off and cast it from you. It is better for you to enter into life lame or maimed, rather than having two hands or two feet, to be cast into the everlasting fire. And if your eye causes you to sin, pluck it out and cast it from you. It is better for you to enter into life with one eye, rather than having two eyes, to be cast into hell fire" (Mt 18.8–9). These metaphors indicate the ruthlessness and decisiveness with which a Christian must destroy sinful tendencies within himself.

The Christian life is the way of spiritual endeavor and struggle. Yet we are not alone in this struggle. God helps us to overcome temptations, to uproot vices within ourselves, and to embark upon the way of virtue, if we turn to him for help, recalling His promise: "Ask, and it will be given to you; seek, and you will find; knock, and it will be opened to you. For everyone who asks receives, and he who seeks finds, and to him who knocks it will be opened" (Mt 7.7–8).

Assignment:

Read the Gospel of Matthew, paying special attention to chapters five to seven (the Sermon on the Mount). Compare your life with the way of life Christ commanded. Ask yourself: Do I want to live as He commanded? If so, then you are on the right path.

The Church and Divine Worship

The Theotokos and the Saints

Prayer

Church Life

The Orthodox Temple

Icons and the Cross

Church Feast Days

The Weekly and Daily Cycles of Divine Worship

The Eucharist

Other Sacraments and Rites

In the first part of the catechism, we spoke about how the Church has two dimensions—earthly and heavenly. An inner unity exists between them, like that between the soul and body in the human person. The heavenly Church, which is triumphant, reveals herself through the earthly Church, which is on a pilgrimage. The life of the Church on earth is a reflection and continuation of her life in the heavens; the heavenly kingdom, thanks to the Church, becomes a reality for earthly people.

Now we will speak about those who make up the heavenly Church and how the earthly Church is structured. We will set forth the necessary minimum that every Christian who embarks upon the path of the Christian life is supposed to know.

1. The Theotokos and the Saints

Christians worship only God, but we also venerate the angels and the saints, those people who have not only been pleasing to God, but who have attained a special spiritual perfection, which we call holiness.

Theotokos.
Mosaic.
Hagia Sophia Cathedral.
Byzantium. 12th c.

The Theotokos

The Most Holy Theotokos stands at the head of the host of saints. The Church venerates her as "more honorable than the cherubim and beyond compare more glorious than the seraphim." This means that she incomparably transcends even the angels in her purity and sanctity. In the person of the Mother of God mankind encounters God who desired to save us: God granted us His Son, while we gave to God the woman who became the greatest exemplar of holiness and perfection. This is stated in one of the hymns for the feast of the Nativity of Christ: "What shall we offer You, O Christ, who for our sakes have appeared on earth as man? Every creature made by You offers You thanks: the angels, a hymn; the heavens, a star; the Wise Men, gifts; the shepherds, their wonder; the earth, its cave; the wilderness, a manger; and we offer You a virgin Mother! O Pre-eternal God, have mercy on us!"[i] Many Church feast days are dedicated to her, and many icons have been painted in her honor. The Most Holy Theotokos intercedes for the human race before her divine Son. Prayers are offered to her at every service, and Christians believe that she hears these prayers and responds to them.

The Angels

Christians also pray to the **angels.**[1] Church doctrine divides the angelic world into various ranks, including the archangels, the cherubim, and the seraphim.[2] Some of the angels are known by name because they are mentioned in the Bible, for example, Gabriel and Michael. A

1 On the angels see page 19.

2 The teaching arose no later than the fifth century that the angelic world is divided into nine ranks comprising three threefold hierarchies. The first and closest to God are the seraphim, cherubim, and thrones; the second are the dominions, authorities, and powers; and the third are the principalities, archangels, and angels. But the Church has never proclaimed this teaching as dogma.

The Annunciation. Fra Angelico. Italy. 1426.

guardian angel is given at birth to every human being. He helps him on his path to God and preserves him from evil.

The Saints

Christians pray to the **saints**. All Christians are called to holiness, but only very few attain it, "For many are called, but few are chosen" (Mt 22.14). Once Jesus was asked: "Lord, are there few who are saved?" And Jesus answered: "Strive to enter through the narrow gate; for many, I say to you, will seek to enter and will not be able" (Lk 13.23–24).

The saints are those who have chosen the "narrow" path that leads to everlasting life, who have travelled this journey to the end, and who have become examples to be emulated for millions of Christians. Through their lives and their endeavors, they have shown that holiness is not an unattainable ideal, but the norm towards which all of the faithful are to direct themselves. Yet the saints did not accomplish their deeds alone: God helped them. To the question: "Who then can be saved?" the Lord answered: "The things which are impossible with men are possible with God" (Lk 18.26–27). Sometimes it would appear that human efforts cannot meet the spiritual and moral demands of Christianity. But the saints have demonstrated that this is not so, and that if we do not rely solely on our own powers but also believe in God and place our hope upon His aid, then "all things are possible to him who believes" (Mk 9.23).

In the church calendar the saints are divided into several categories in accordance with the time when they lived, their way of life, and the rank they enjoyed. A difference is made between the saints of the Old Testament and the saints who shone forth during the time of the New Testament.

First of all, among the Old Testament saints, we remember the **righteous** men and women whose stories are told on the pages of the Bible, such as Abraham, Isaac, Jacob, Moses, King David, and others. The Christian Church venerates the **prophets** Elijah and Elisha, whose narratives are also found in the Bible, as well as those prophets whose books have become a part of the Bible: Isaiah, Jeremiah, Ezekiel, Daniel, and the twelve

The fiery ascent of the holy prophet Elijah. Detail of an icon. Russia. 18 c.

The twelve apostles. Icon. 14th c.

"minor prophets." The chain of Old Testament prophets concluded with John the Baptist, who stood at the threshold of the New Testament and whose name opens the list of Christian saints (he is sometimes called the last prophet and the first Christian martyr).

The Church venerates the **apostles**—the immediate disciples of Christ, chosen by Him to minister. According to the Gospels, Jesus chose twelve apostles (Mt 10.1–5; Mk 3.13–19; Lk 6.13–16), and then the other seventy (Lk 10.1). Of the twelve apostles, one became a traitor, and after Christ's Resurrection his place was taken by another (Acts 1.15–26). Then, in a miraculous way, the Lord called Paul, who before had been a persecutor of the Church (Acts 9.1–20). The Apostles Peter and Paul are venerated as "chief among the apostles," while the other apostles—from both the twelve and the seventy—are also widely venerated in the Church. The Church especially glorifies the four evangelists—Matthew and John, who were from among the twelve apostles; and Mark and Luke, who were from among the seventy.

The veneration of **martyrs** has been attested in the Church from the beginning. Many of the apostles, including Peter and Paul, died a martyr's death. The first three centuries in the history of the Christian Church were a period of persecution, when martyrdom was a heroic feat on a wide scale. Persecution of the Church has been renewed from time to time, up to the present. The twentieth century gave the world a whole host of martyrs, who testified to their faithfulness to Christ by undergoing the severest afflictions and torments. Among the ancient martyrs, particularly, are George the Trophy-Bearer,

Saint Nicholas the Wonderworker. Icon donated in 1327 by the Serbian Tsar Stephen III (Uros) to the Basilica of St Nicholas. Bari, Italy.

Demetrius of Thessalonica, and Theodore of Amasea, whose names are borne by many Christians.

Confessors are those saints who courageously endured torments for Christ, but who remained alive and died a natural death.

The **holy hierarchs** are those saints who were bishops. Among them, particularly, are St Nicholas of Myra in Lycia (also called St Nicholas the Wonderworker) who lived in the fourth century, and his contemporaries Athanasius of Alexandria, Basil the Great, Gregory the Theologian, and John Chrysostom, and many other holy hierarchs in the following centuries. Those bishops and priests who died a martyr's death are called "hieromartyrs."

The "**venerable**" are the saints who were monastics and who were glorified for their ascetic way of life, spiritual insight, and ability to work miracles, as well as other spiritual gifts. Among them are the founders of monasticism Anthony the Great, Pachomius the Wise, Macarius the Great, and Hilarion the Great, who lived in the fourth century; the founders of western monasticism, John Cassian and Benedict of Nursia in the fifth and sixth centuries; as well as the founders of Russian monasticism Anthony and Theodosius of the Caves in Kiev (eleventh century) and saints of a later period such as Sergius of Radonezh, Seraphim of Sarov, and Silouan of Athos. Those monks who died a martyr's death are known as "venerable martyrs."

"**Holy fools**" are those saints who performed a special type of spiritual feat in their life—they assumed the guise of insanity in order to subject themselves to insults and disgrace from people. This façade concealed great spiritual gifts, including the gift of prophecy. The most famous Byzantine holy fool was Andrew, who is known through his association with the feast day of the Protecting Veil of the Theotokos.[3] The most renowned Russian holy fool was Basil the Blessed, whose name is linked with the famous cathedral on Red Square in Moscow. The blessed Xenia of Petersburg also enjoys widespread veneration.[4]

Among the saints there are many **kings** and **queens, right-believing princes** and **princesses**. Some of these have been canonized for their personal holiness, while some for those noble deeds that they did for the Church. Thus, for example, the emperor Constantine the Great (fourth century) was canonized mainly as the person through whom the Christian Church received freedom after three centuries of persecution. The holy Great Prince Vladimir of Kiev (tenth and eleventh centuries) is venerated as the baptizer of Old Russia. Both of these saints have been glorified as "**Equal-to-the-Apostles**": the Church thus ranks their deeds as part of apostolic ministry.

The **passion-bearers** are those saints who were not martyrs for Christ, but who were likened to Him through their patient acceptance of sufferings and death. The right-believing Princes Boris and Gleb (eleventh century), are particularly venerated as passion-bearers. The Royal Passion-bearers are the last Russian Emperor Nicholas II and his wife and children, who were shot in 1918.

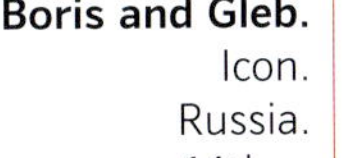

The faithful princes Boris and Gleb. Icon. Russia. 14th c.

The saints abide with God in the kingdom of heaven in everlasting blessedness, yet they do no forsake their earthly brothers and sisters: they listen to their prayers, come to their aid and intercede for them before God.

3 For this feast day see pages 220–221.

4 The word "blessed" is also used for saints who were not holy fools, for example, for some theologians of the period of the Ecumenical Councils (the blessed Augustine and the blessed Jerome in the west, the blessed Theodoret in the east). Matrona of Moscow is also called "blessed," although she was renowned not in the main for being a holy fool.

Ten Categories of Saints

As the Church teaches, every person is created in the image and likeness of God. As a result of the fall, the image of God in man was distorted. The goal of a Christian's life is to restore the image of God in oneself, to become like God.

In the New Covenant, all Christians who are united with God by the grace of the Holy Spirit are called saints. Since the first centuries of its existence, the Church has venerated saints. Currently, in order to glorify and venerate a deceased person as a saint canonization is required. For local veneration of an ascetic, permission from the patriarch is required; for church-wide recognition of a saint, a decision of the Council of Bishops is required. The grounds for canonization may be: holiness of life, suffering for the faith, the gift of miracles, outstanding contribution to the cause of Christian education.

Formally, we can distinguish ten categories of holiness.

1. Apostles

Twelve disciples of Christ, called by Him personally, the other seventy of His closest followers, and the Apostle Paul, mysteriously chosen by the Savior after His Ascension. The Apostles Peter and Paul are revered as the most important apostles. The Apostles became the first preachers of the New Testament, the founders of the first Churches. The main testimony about the life of Christ, the Gospel, was recorded by the Apostles and Evangelists Matthew, Mark, Luke, and John.

Evangelists are often depicted with a book—the Gospel.

2. Martyrs

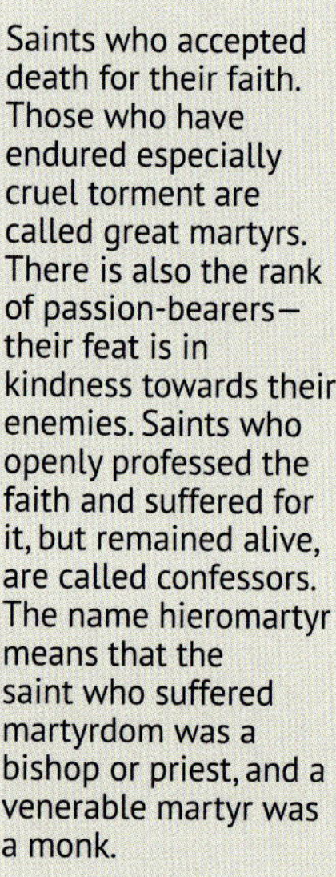

Saints who accepted death for their faith. Those who have endured especially cruel torment are called great martyrs. There is also the rank of passion-bearers—their feat is in kindness towards their enemies. Saints who openly professed the faith and suffered for it, but remained alive, are called confessors. The name hieromartyr means that the saint who suffered martyrdom was a bishop or priest, and a venerable martyr was a monk.

The martyr is depicted on the icon in a red chiton. Often in his hands he has a cross or an instrument of his torment.

3. Righteous

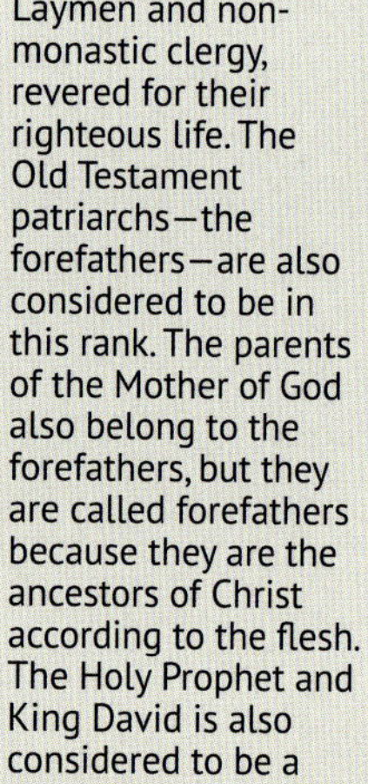

Laymen and non-monastic clergy, revered for their righteous life. The Old Testament patriarchs—the forefathers—are also considered to be in this rank. The parents of the Mother of God also belong to the forefathers, but they are called forefathers because they are the ancestors of Christ according to the flesh. The Holy Prophet and King David is also considered to be a forefather.

4. Venerable

Monastics revered for their ascetic life

They are depicted in monastic robes and their right hand is often held in blessing.

5. Holy Hierarchs

Bishops who were known for their righteous life and pastoral care for their diocese, for the preservation of Orthodoxy from heresies and schisms.

They are depicted in full liturgical episcopal vestments.

6. Right-Believing

Kings and queens, right-believing princes and princesses are glorified in the rank of the faithful for pious lives, works of mercy, strengthening the Church and faith.

They are often depicted with royal crowns and regal clothes.

7. Prophets

The prophets communicated the will of God to Israel and announced to the chosen people the coming Messiah. The Church honors eighteen Old Testament prophets and one New Testament prophet, Saint John the Baptist.

In icons, a prophet most often holds in his hands a scroll with the text of his prophecy.

8. Wonderworkers

Factually, miracleworkers are not a truly a separate category, since many saints possessed the gift of miracles, and miracleworking is one of the conditions for canonization.

9. Equal-to-the-Apostles

Saints, like the apostles, labored in converting entire countries and peoples.

In iconography they are often shown holding a cross—a symbol of Baptism.

10. Holy Fools, blessed

Having voluntarily taken upon themselves the image of madmen, holy fools denounced acquisitiveness for Christ's sake. According to tradition, some saints are also called blessed, for example, Jerome, Augustine, Matrona, and others.

Holy fools are most often depicted in shabby clothes.

11. Unmercenaries

Christians, famous for their selflessness, renunciation of wealth for the sake of their faith. Usually these include saints who had the gift of healing and did not take payment for their work.

The unmercenaries are most often depicted with medicine boxes.

Venerating relics of saints.

The Relics of Saints

Relics are the bodily remains of saints. Often the bodies of saints remain incorrupt for many years and even centuries (although incorruptibility is not necessarily a sign of sanctity, in the same way that sanctity does not necessarily entail incorruptibility).

The relics of saints, regardless of the degree of their preservation, are venerated as holy objects: the faithful kiss them and ask the saints for their help and for healing. The basis for this veneration is the belief that the grace that the saints received renewed not only their souls, but also their bodies.

The relics of many saints have been preserved intact and repose in the churches or places where the saints lived during their life on earth. Particles are taken from some relics to be given to other places and churches.

The Heavenly Protector

According to the tradition of the Orthodox Church, every newly-baptized Christian receives the name of a

Guardian Angel. Icon. Russia. 17th c.

particular saint. In some other local Orthodox Churches (for example, the Serbian Church), there is no such tradition. As a rule, this name corresponds to our given name but in some instances it can be different from it.

The saint whose name was given to us in the sacrament of Baptism becomes our **heavenly protector**. The feast day of this saint is called "name day" or "saint's day." This saint is not to be confused with the guardian angel whom God assigns to every person.

The Veneration of the Saints in the Orthodox Church

Sometimes the Orthodox Church is criticized for viewing the saints as mediators between man and God, when it should be possible to communicate with God without mediators. This, of course, is an unfounded criticism. The Church recognizes the experience of direct communication with God. Moreover, she views it as the foundation of the spiritual life of every Christian. But she does not believe that the veneration of the saints can in any way hinder direct prayerful communication between a person and God. Most of the prayers said by Orthodox Christians in church or at home are addressed to God. Nevertheless, the Christian also prays to the Theotokos and the saints.

For the Orthodox Christian, the saints are living bearers of true Christianity whose lives serve as a lofty moral example. The Church, moreover, believes that the saints, even after departing this life, continue to live in the Church. It is upon this belief in their living presence that our prayers addressed to them are founded.

---

[i] Last sticheron at "Lord, I call" at Vespers on Christmas Eve; OCA translation.

2. Prayer

Prayer is above all **communion with God**. Prayer takes the form of a discourse or conversation: it has a verbal expression.

Prayer is always a **dialogue**: it contains not only the words that the Christian addresses to God, but also God's response. Prayer is not a one-way street: it is the movement of God and the human person towards each other.

To hear God, to sense the Father within himself, to feel His presence in one's life is the true goal of prayer. God's response may come in many different forms, but the sincere and heartfelt prayer of the Christian is never left unanswered.

The Lord's Prayer

Jesus Christ taught His followers to call God their Father and to pray to Him using the following words:

Our Father, who art in heaven, hallowed be Thy name.
Thy kingdom come.
Thy will be done on earth as it is in heaven.
Give us this day our daily bread.
And forgive us our debts, as we forgive our debtors.
And lead us not into temptation, but deliver us from the evil one. (Mt 6.9–13)[1]

In the Christian Church, this prayer is known as the Lord's Prayer. It is read (or sung) at all the services, and Christians use it when turning to God in their prayers at home.

In the first three petitions of the prayer the word "Thy" (archaic form for "you" when addressing one person) dominates. In the following three petitions the word "we" dominates. In turning to God the Father, we beseech Him in the Lord's Prayer that His name be hallowed (that is, be glorified) according to His nature, that His kingdom become a reality in our lives, that His will be done for us as it is done in the angelic world. We ask of God our daily sustenance; we ask of Him forgiveness of sins and deliverance from temptation and the power of the devil.

Lord's Prayer for the apostles and the Church. Detail of a miniature. Byzantium. 11th c.

How to Pray Correctly

Sometimes people say: "I don't pray because I don't know how to pray." Or: "I don't pray because I don't know the liturgical language." In fact, in order to pray to God, it is not necessary to know any language apart from the one in which we speak and think. In church a particular liturgical language may be used for services, but for personal prayer this is not necessary. We can communicate with God in the same way as we communicate with our parents, children, and those close to us. The most important thing is that our prayer be sincere, reverential, and heartfelt.

It is possible to pray in any place at any time. In the usual domestic setting, as well as in church, a Christian prays standing, looking at the icons, and **crossing himself**. In order to do so, the first three fingers of the right

[1] In the Orthodox tradition when a layperson reads the Our Father, he omits the concluding doxology ("For Thine is the kingdom, and the power, and the glory. Amen."). But a priest ends the prayer with: "For Thine is the kingdom, and the power, and the glory, of the Father, and of the Son, and of the Holy Spirit, now and ever, and unto ages of ages. Amen."

hand are brought together, and the two smaller fingers are pressed into the palm of the hand, and then as we pray we touch our forehead, stomach, right shoulder, and then left shoulder.[2] But there can be special circumstances when we can pray sitting (for example, on public transport), and even lying down (for example, if we are in bed because of illness). In this instance, we can refrain from all outward signs of prayer and pray in our minds and hearts without opening our mouths.

The Jesus Prayer

The **Jesus Prayer** has been used in the Orthodox Church since ancient times. It exists in its full form—"Lord Jesus Christ, Son of God, have mercy upon me, the sinner"—and in shortened versions, for example: "Lord Jesus Christ, have mercy upon me," or "Son of God, have mercy upon me." This prayer, or even its shorter version—"Lord, have mercy" (which can often be heard at the services)—can be said to oneself. The repetition of this prayer helps us to be constantly aware of God's presence.

The Apostle Paul encourages us thus: "Rejoice always, pray without ceasing, in everything give thanks" (1 Thess 5.16–18). First of all, these words describe the Christian life as filled with the constant joy of sensing God's presence. Second, the Christian is called upon to **pray ceaselessly** and not only from time to time: this ideal has found its embodiment in the practice of the Jesus Prayer. Third, the Christian is to thank God for all things: not only for successes and joys, but also for the afflictions and sufferings that God sends him in order to test his faith and patience.

[2] In the tradition of the Old Rite, which has been retained in Old Rite parishes, two fingers (the index and middle fingers) are brought together, while the thumb is joined to the third and little fingers, hence making the sign of the cross primarily with two fingers.

Polar explorers gather for prayer in the Church of the Holy Trinity on Waterloo Island, Antarctica.

Prayer of Thanksgiving, Repentance, and Supplication

Depending upon its content, prayer can be of thanksgiving, repentance, or supplication.

Quite often we attribute to our own capabilities and labors the successes that we would not have achieved had it not been for God's help. Often we do not see God, who ceaselessly cares for us, in the events of our lives. It is very important to be able to **give thanks to God** for His good deeds and to learn how to see His participation in our lives.

Many prayers composed by the saints have a **penitential nature**. The Christian, every time he goes to sleep, is to recall the past day and ask God to forgive any mistakes that have been committed. At the first available opportunity he should speak about these mistakes in Confession.

Prayer of supplication can have a quite varied content. We can ask for help in our spiritual lives, as well as for all sorts of material needs. One ought not to be afraid of turning to God even for the most insignificant of needs. But prayer should not be viewed merely as a means for attaining certain material goods. In prayer, our standing before God and communion with Him are most important.

Prayer for Others

A Christian is to pray not only for himself, but also **for his neighbors**—his parents, children, relatives, friends, co-workers, superiors, and those under him. Church history knows many instances when the prayer of a mother saved her children from death, when a gravely ill husband's health was restored thanks to the ardent prayers of his wife when the doctor had said that his illness was terminal. Prayer for those around us is an effective method of rendering help, and one of the good deeds that do not require any material sacrifices, but only the loving disposition of the heart.

Jesus Christ calls upon His followers to pray not only for those close to them, but also for those who have **offended and persecuted them** (Mt 5.43–44). Prayer is the universal response to human anger, enmity, and hatred. Very often people think that evil can be conquered only by using evil in return. But Christ teaches us differently: evil is vanquished by good. And prayer is the powerful means used for this victory. Thanks to prayer for our enemies we expel from our hearts enmity and hatred towards them, and this is already an important stage on the path to reconciliation.

Christians pray not only for the living, but also **for the dead**. This prayer is important, first, for those who have

departed for the other world and whose posthumous fate is being decided by God. Every person on earth is connected with many other people by the bonds of kinship, love, friendship, and professional interaction. And as we have compassion for those around us in this life, so we ought to have compassion for them when they leave us.

Prayer for the departed, moreover, is important for us who remain here on earth. It helps us to overcome the loss of a loved one and not to lose our connection with him or her. This connection will be fully restored after we enter into eternity to be with them.

The Canon of St Andrew at St Vladimir's Orthodox Theological Seminary.

Prayer Should Not Be Ostentatious

The Lord Jesus Christ said to His disciples: "And when you pray, you shall not be like the hypocrites. For they love to pray standing in the synagogues and on the corners of the streets, that they may be seen by men. Assuredly, I say to you, they have their reward. But you, when you pray, go into your room, and when you have shut your door, pray to your Father who is in the secret place; and your Father who sees in secret will reward you openly. And when you pray, do not use vain repetitions as the heathen do. For they think that they will be heard for their many words. Therefore do not be like them. For your Father knows the things you have need of before you ask Him" (Mt 6.5–8).

The advice to say little in prayer does not mean that prayer cannot be lengthy. Jesus Himself spent whole nights in prayer (Mt 18.22–25; Lk 6.12), and the first Christian prayer gatherings often lasted from evening to morning (Acts 20.7–11). The Savior's words indicate that in prayer we ought to avoid extraneous words—that is, we are to concentrate on what is most important.

In reminding us that prayer should not be hypocritical or ostentatious, the Lord at the same time points towards God's omniscience—to the fact that God knows beforehand everything that we will ask of Him.

Why Is It Necessary to Pray?

Often people ask: why is it necessary to pray if God knows everything that we want to say to Him? We pray not in order to convey to God what *He* does not know: we pray in order to share with Him what is important to *us*, what pains us. And God always hears our petitions. Our lives consist not only of that which God has willed for us, but also what we wish to ask of God. Life, ultimately, is the fruit of a joint creative endeavor between the human person and God.

The goal of a Christian's life lies in uniting his personal human will fully with God's will. Thus, the petition "**Thy will be done**" reflects the disposition that informs all our prayer. We can ask of God anything that we want, but ultimately we must entrust ourselves to the will of God, recalling that God knows what we need better than we do ourselves.

It is for this reason that we do not always receive from God what we ask of Him. If we pray and do not receive what we have asked for, this does not mean that God does not hear us: He hears us, but decides differently. Trust in God helps us to overcome God's silence when it appears that He does not want to help us. Like parents who listen to their children's demands, but do not always respond to them, God always listens to us, but does not always respond in the way that we would expect.

When communicating with God, we must be prepared for both surprises and disappointments. Yet the cause of these disappointments is not God's inability to fulfill our petitions, but our lack of desire to understand that if He has not fulfilled them, then we should accept this as His holy will.

3. Church Life

The word "Church" is used in relation to both the One, Holy, Catholic, and Apostolic Church (in this instance it is written with a capital letter) and in relation to the concrete church building (in which case it is written with a lower case letter).

Church Life

People's acquaintance with the church building is often limited to entering it for particular occasions—to baptize a child, to hold a funeral service for the departed, to have a prayer service for someone who is gravely ill, to light a candle before taking a test, and so on. All of this in itself is important, but participation in church life should not be confined to this.

Church life presupposes regular participation—at least on Sundays and major feast days—in the services and **Holy Communion**. The life of the Orthodox Christian is structured not only around the calendar of secular holidays, weekdays, and events in one's personal, professional, and family life, but also around the church calendar. And the church for him is not only a place that he will drop in on the way to or from work, or which he attends only on special occasions, but is the place where he regularly goes to encounter God and to communicate with other members of the church community.

Love of God's Church

In the Psalms it is said: "One thing have I asked of the Lord, this will I seek: that I may dwell in the house of the Lord all the days of my life, to behold the delights of the Lord, and to visit His holy temple" (Ps 26.4). These words express the feelings of a soul that loves God and strives to commune with Him.

The **church is God's dwelling-place**: "The Lord is in His holy temple" (Ps 10.4). People go to church not because "one ought to" or because "it is required." The natural state of a Christian's soul is to head for God's church, to love worship and prayer. Like the psalmist of old, who said: "I was glad when they said unto me, 'Let us go into the house of the Lord'" (Ps 121.1), a Christian rejoices when he hears the ringing of a church bell announcing the start of worship and willingly puts aside his everyday affairs in order to go to church.

4. The Orthodox Temple

The Orthodox temple, or church building, is the place where Christians worship, where people commune with God through prayer and the Church's sacraments.

The Architecture of an Orthodox Church Building

Churches can be made of wood, stone, or other materials. They can differ greatly from each other in their external appearance. Ideally, the architecture of Orthodox church buildings would include a dome and cross (or several domes with crosses), although in small parishes this is not always possible, and in many places new to Orthodoxy church buildings follow local architectural customs for places of worship. The Orthodox church building can almost always be distinguished from other buildings that do not have a religious function. Many churches have a bell tower adjoining them.

Orthodox churches, with rare exceptions, are built facing east. This has deep meaning: the east symbolizes Christ, who in theological and liturgical texts is referred

Churches in the town of Gorokhovets, Russia

to as the "Sun of righteousness" (Mal 4.2) and the "Orient from on high" (Lk 1.78 Douay).

The interior of the church, as a rule, is divided into three parts: the sanctuary, the nave, and the narthex. Sometimes the division between the narthex and the nave is not architecturally obvious. But the division between the sanctuary and the nave is always delineated by a barrier, most often in the form of an iconostasis.

Orthodox Church

An Orthodox church is a building or room especially dedicated to God, where public worship, sacraments, and rituals are performed.

History

The first Christian churches were built in Byzantium during the reign of Emperor Constantine the Great (fourth c.). Before this, services were performed in secret in the homes of Christians, in caves, catacombs, as well as in public meeting houses (basilicas).

In Rus', the first stone church was erected in Kiev in 996, during the reign of the holy Equal-to-the-Apostles Prince Vladimir. It was called Tithes, since Saint Vladimir allocated a tenth of his income—a tithe—for its construction and maintenance.

Types of Churches

There are several types of church buildings, each with its own symbolic meaning.

1. Cruciform

Based on the cross symbolizing the cross of Christ, through which mankind escapes the power of sin.

2. Elongated

This type is based on a quadrilateral shape, a symbol of the completeness of the world gathered in the Church.

3. Circular

It is based on a circle, a symbol of the fullness of the Church and her inseparable connection with the eternal God.

4. Ship

This architectural type is characterized by the arrangement of parts of the temple—the vestibule with the bell tower and the refectory, the central part and the altar—elongated in one line. It symbolizes the Church as a ship of salvation.

5. Star shaped

The second tier of such a temple has the shape of an eight-pointed "Bethlehem" star, a guide for people to God.

6. Churches of mixed shapes

These combine the architectural features of different types of temples.

It is possible to overlay or combine several forms.

Exterior of the church

Churches can differ in their external structure, but general principles of construction are observed.

1. Apse

A recess on the eastern side of the church. Most often it has a semicircular shape. The altar is located in the apse.

2. Cube

The primary part of the church.

3. Zakomara (the gable)

A feature of Russian church architecture. A semicircular or keeled completion of part of the outer wall of the temple.

4. Drum

The upper part of the church, over which a dome is built, topped with a cross. As a rule, drums have the shape of a cylinder or prism.

5. Cupola (Dome)

At the top of the church, a structure over the drum, crowned by a cross. Most often in the Russian tradition, the dome has the shape of an onion. The number of domes may be different, but each of them has its own meaning: two domes mean the two natures in Jesus Christ, Divine and Human; three—the three Persons of the Holy Trinity; five—Jesus Christ and the four evangelists; seven—the seven sacraments and the seven Ecumenical Councils; nine are the nine ranks of angels; thirteen are Jesus Christ and the twelve apostles. Rarely there may there may be even more domes.

6. Bell tower

A special high extension to the temple (usually above the entrance), at the top of which there is a belfry.

7. Portal

Architecturally decorated entrance to the temple.

8. Porch

An open or closed porch in front of the entrance to the temple, elevated in relation to the ground level.

The Iconostasis

The **iconostasis** is a wall with icons. Iconostases can be made up of many tiers or a single tier. A single-tiered iconostasis is thus made up of a single row of icons. In the center of the iconostasis are the holy doors (often called "royal doors"), which are closed when there is no service in the church but which are opened at certain moments during worship. To the right of the holy doors is an icon of Jesus Christ, and to the left an icon of the Theotokos holding the infant Christ. Further in this row (the "local row") there may be an icon of the saint or feast day to which the church is dedicated, and other icons that have importance for this particular church. Apart from the holy doors, in the lower row of the iconostasis there are the north (to the left) door and the south (to the right) door: they are used to enter the sanctuary during worship and when there is no service.

If the iconostasis consists of many tiers, the second tier includes images of the most important church feasts (the so-called "festal row"), the third tier includes images of the Savior, the Mother of God, and the apostles (the so-called "*Deisis* row"),[1] the fourth row the prophets (the "prophets' row"), and the fifth row the righteous saints of the Old Testament (the "forefathers' row").

The subjects of the icons in the iconostasis can vary in different churches, but the general meaning of the

[1] From the Greek meaning "prayerful supplication." It denotes images with the Savior in the center and with the Theotokos to the left and John the Baptist to the right.

iconostasis is the same everywhere—it is not simply a barrier between the sanctuary and the nave, but a window to the other world: gazing down upon us through the icons from eternity are the faces of the Savior, the Mother of God, and the saints.

The Sanctuary (or Altar) and Its Elements

The **sanctuary** (often called the "**altar**") is intended primarily for clergy (bishops, priests, and deacons) and servers (readers, subdeacons, and altar servers) who participate in worship. Only those who have a blessing may enter the sanctuary, and only the clergy are permitted to touch the altar and stand in front of it.

The **altar** is a table located in the center of the sanctuary. The priest stands before it during the service, and the Holy Gifts—the bread and wine intended for the Eucharist—are placed upon it. The book of the Gospels lies upon the altar, which at special moments during services is carried out of the sanctuary to be read and to be venerated by the faithful. An **antimension** also lies upon the altar—a special cloth signed by the bishop (this signature shows that the church belongs to a certain diocese and that the priests of that church have the blessing of the bishop to celebrate the services). According to the custom of the Orthodox Church, a particle of the relics of a martyr or saint is sewn into the antimension. This reflects the ancient tradition of celebrating the Liturgy on the tombs of the martyrs. The same tradition is also reflected in the way a particle

Iconostasis

Iconostasis is a partition with rows (ranks) of icons, separating the altar from the main part of the temple. The modern classic five-tier iconostasis was formed in Rus' in the fifteenth to sixteenth centuries. The ranks of the five-tiered iconostasis are arranged in tiers, one above the other.

1. Royal (Holy) doors

Symbolize the entrance into the kingdom of God. The icons depict the Annunciation (symbol of the beginning of the New Testament) and either the four evangelists or the saints who compiled the Liturgy, Saints John Chrysostom and Basil the Great.

2. Mystical Supper

The Eucharist takes the central place in the service, which is celebrated in the image of the Last Supper.

3. Jesus Christ, Pantocrator

If the altar is consecrated in honor of an event in the life of the Savior, then this particular icon will be located here.

4. Virgin and Child

If the altar is consecrated in honor of a specific icon of the Theotokos, or an event from her life, then this icon is placed here.

5. Deacon doors

Deacon doors typically have icons of archangels, the protomartyrs Archdeacons Stephen and Lawrence, or Moses and Aaron. The northern door may depict the wise thief.

6. Locally revered icon

7. Patron saint of the parish

Depicts a saint or holiday in whose honor the temple was consecrated.

8. Twelve major feasts

Icons of the Twelve Great Feasts—the main events in the life of Christ and the Theotokos. The icons are arranged in the order they appear in the church year, starting from September 1, or in chronological order. The first (on the left) in both chronological and liturgical order is the icon of the Nativity of the Theotokos, followed by (chronologically): Entry of the Theotokos into the Temple, Annunciation, Nativity of Christ, Theophany, Transfiguration, Raising of Lazarus, Entry into Jerusalem, Crucifixion, Resurrection of Christ, Ascension, Pentecost, Dormition of the Theotokos (this icon, in any sequence, will be on the far right). Often the series includes the Exaltation of the Cross, Pokrov, and other feasts. The icons of the feasts and the Deisis can change places.

9. Deisis

The main row of the iconostasis. Main theme: the second coming of Christ in glory and the prayer of the saints for humanity ("Deisis"—prayer). In the center of the rank is the Savior on the throne. On the right and left are icons of those praying to Christ: on the left are the Theotokos, Archangel Michael, and the Apostle Peter.
On the right are John the Baptist, Archangel Gabriel, and the Apostle Paul. This is followed by icons of saints or the twelve apostles.

10. Old Testament prophets and patriarchs

Icons of the Old Testament prophets who testified about Christ: Kings David and Solomon, Prophets Elijah, Zechariah, Daniel, Ezekiel, and others. In the center is the icon of the Mother of God "The Sign" as a symbol of the fulfillment of all prophecies.

11. Forefathers

This rank depicts the Old Testament righteous who lived before Moses, through whom God gave the Law. There may be icons of Adam, Eve, Abel, Abraham, Isaac, Jacob, Noah, and Melchizedek.

12. Completion

The Crucifixion Icon or Cross is a symbol of the Savior's atoning sacrifice.

Altar

An altar (Latin for "high") is a sacred place for offering sacrifice to God. In the church the altar symbolizes heaven. The main thing in the altar is the holy table, on which the main sacrament of the Church is celebrated, the Eucharist. The altar is oriented to the east. Sunrise is a symbol of light and one of the images of Christ.

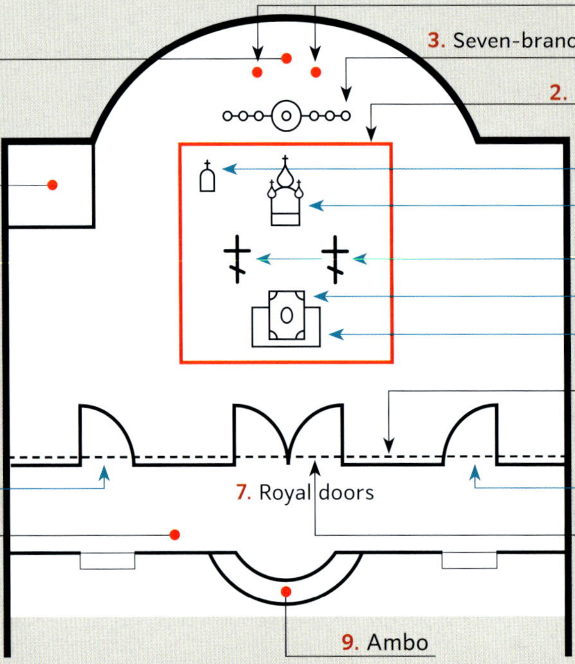

4. Processional cross and icons

1. High place

3. Seven-branched candelabrum

2. Holy (Altar) Table

5. Table of Oblation

(chalice, discos, spear, star, covers, Eucharistic spoon)

Ciborium

Tabernacle

The Cross

The Gospel

Antimension

6. Iconostasis

North doors

South doors

7. Royal doors

10. Soleas

8. Curtains

9. Ambo

1 **High place**—the farthest, eastern part of the altar. The bishop sits on a seat built on a high place at certain moments of the bishop's service, and the clergy serving with him are located on the sides. In ordinary parish churches, on a high place there is symbolically the throne of the bishop or there is a lamp or a tall candle, and on the sides there are benches for priests. The high place symbolizes the vision of John the Theologian: the Lord sitting on the throne, and next to Him sat kings and priests (Rev. 4.4).

2 **Holy Table**—a table standing in the center of the altar opposite the royal doors. The sacrament of the Eucharist is celebrated on the altar, and sacred objects are also located: an antimension (a rectangular cloth depicting the position of Christ in the tomb and a particle of relics sewn into it) with the signature of the ruling bishop, the Gospel, altar crosses, and a tabernacle. The spare Holy Gifts are kept in the tabernacle. Thus, the Lord Himself is constantly present in the temple.

3 Seven-branched candelabrum—a special candelabrum with seven lamps. The seven-branched candlestick stands on the altar opposite the royal doors, or separately, immediately behind the altar. Initially, the seven-branched candlestick was in the tabernacle of meeting, and then in the Jerusalem temple. The seven-branched candlestick symbolizes the seven spirits of God from the vision of the Apostle John the Theologian (Rev. 4.5), the fullness of the gifts of the Holy Spirit, and the seven sacraments of the Church.

4 Processional cross—a large portable cross with a depiction of the Crucifixion. During the cross procession,

the altar cross is taken out of the altar. An external icon of the Mother of God is located symmetrically with the altar cross. The altar cross is located behind the throne opposite the royal doors at the high place, at the right corner of the throne and the icon of the Mother of God at the left. Often the processional cross is placed centrally, just to the east of the seven-branched candlestick.

5 Table of oblation—a table at the north wall of the altar, to the left of the altar. Proskomedia is performed on the altar—that is, bread and wine are prepared for the Eucharist. Sacred vessels for celebrating the Eucharist are kept on or near the altar.

6 Iconostasis—a wall of several rows of icons spanning the entire width of the temple, separating the altar. To enter the altar, there are three doors in the iconostasis: the royal doors and the northern and southern deacon doors.

7 Royal doors—symbolize the doors of heaven.

8 Curtains—the curtain behind the iconostasis separating the royal doors and the altar. During services it opens and closes. The veil can be of different colors depending on the season. In the Old Testament temple, a curtain separated the Holy of Holies from the temple. During the death of the Savior on the cross, the veil of the Jerusalem temple was torn in two as a sign that heaven was now open to all who follow Christ.

9 High place—a semicircular elevation far to the east of the iconostasis opposite the royal doors. The Gospel is read on the ambo, litanies and sermons are pronounced.

10 Soleas—elevation in front of the iconostasis across the entire width of the temple.

of a martyr's or saint's relics is placed within the altar when it is consecrated.

The **table of oblation**, upon which the priest prepares the bread and the wine for the Eucharist, is located on the left side of the sanctuary.

Behind the altar (sometimes upon the altar) there is a **seven-branched candelabrum**. It is a reminder of one of the details of the Old Testament tabernacle[2] (Ex 25.31–37) and the Temple in Jerusalem.

The Nave

In front of the iconostasis there is the **solea**—a raised platform upon which the clergy go in procession during the services. The central part of the solea is called the **ambo**. It is from here that the priest delivers a sermon. At each end of the solea is a space referred to as a "**kliros**" or "choir" where singers gather during worship services.[3]

The church walls may be decorated with frescos depicting various events in the sacred history of the Old and New Testaments, images of the saints, and scenes from the lives of the saints. The content of the frescos, as a rule, relates to the event or saint to which the church is dedicated. The images in the frescos are placed in rows as on the iconostasis.

In addition to the main sanctuary, there may be side-sanctuaries in the church located in the same part as the main sanctuary, or they may be separate constructions within the nave of the church. These sanctuaries are sometimes referred to as **side-chapels**, and so we speak

[2] The "tabernacle" or "tent" was a portable temple used in ancient Israel before the Temple of Jerusalem was built.

[3] Some churches have singers on two klirosy, some on only one; and in some churches there is a choir loft.

of the main sanctuary and the side-sanctuaries or side-chapels of a church.

The architecture and the interior of the church remind the faithful of the invisible world that exists beyond the confines of the visible world. When Christian architecture and liturgical aesthetics came into being, many of the faithful could not read, and the images on the walls and icons were viewed as a "Gospel for the illiterate": the priest would point towards them as he told the story of a particular saint or event in Scripture. Today everyone is able to read, but the sacred images have not lost any of their meaning as a result.

5. Icons and the Cross

By nature God is spirit (Jn 4.24) and He is invisible. But the main event of Christian history was the incarnation of God—the coming into the world of God in human flesh. In the incarnation "the Word became flesh" (Jn 1.14), and thus in the face of the Son of God, Jesus Christ, people could contemplate the mysterious and invisible divine countenance.

It is precisely upon this truth that the theory and practice of icon-painting is founded. The invisible God cannot be depicted, but we can depict what was revealed to people in its visible aspect. It is possible, therefore, to portray Jesus Christ and the events of His life. In the icon of the Theophany it is possible to depict the Holy Spirit in the way He appeared to people when Jesus emerged from the waters of the Jordan—that is, in the form of a dove. And we can portray in icons the Mother of God, the saints, and various events of sacred history and the history of the Church.

The Veneration of Icons

In the Orthodox Church icons are paid a special veneration. The veneration of icons is not merely an ancient tradition: it is a dogma. The proclamation of this dogma in the eighth century came about as a result of the the iconoclasts' ferocious persecution of those who venerated the icons. The Church condemned iconoclasm as a heresy and articulated the theological understanding of the practice of painting and venerating icons. This practice has been a part of church life since the earliest times.

The veneration of icons has nothing in common with idolatry and is in no way a violation of the second commandment of the Law of Moses: "You shall not make for yourself an idol" (Ex 20.4 NASB). This commandment was aimed against the worship of false gods, since the ancients were inclined to deify animals, everyday objects, or the powers of nature, and to worship them as gods. Christians, on the contrary, worship the one true God.

In responding to the attacks of the iconoclasts, the Church Fathers insisted on the difference between **worship**, which is due to God alone, and **veneration**, which befits the Theotokos and the saints. Christians worship the one God glorified in the Trinity. They venerate the saints, but do not deify them or worship them as gods or idols.

Prayer in front of the Robe of the Mother of God in Zugdidi, Georgia.

The veneration of icons is expressed in the way the faithful pray before them, prostrate themselves before them, and kiss them. These signs of respect, however, are not directed towards the painted board, but to the one depicted on it. As the Church Fathers said: "The honor of the image passes over to the archetype."[i]

The Theological, Liturgical, and Moral Significance of Icons

Icons can substantially differ from one another in style, but the factor that distinguishes all icons from other painted works is that they are created in accordance with a "canon"—a set of rules that have remained inviolable throughout the centuries.

The icon is not a portrait, it does not claim to give a precise rendering of the outward appearance of a particular saint. We do not know how the saints looked in antiquity, but we do have photographs of people whom the Church has canonized as saints in recent times. The comparison of a photograph with an icon of the saint visually demonstrates that the icon painter strives to preserve only the most general characteristics of the outward appearance of the saint. On the icon he is recognizable, but he is also different: his features are sharper, ennobled; they have an iconic aspect.

The icon manifests the human person in his transfigured, deified state: "The icon is the image of the man in whom the grace which consumes passions and which sanctifies everything is truly present. This is why his flesh is represented completely differently from ordinary corruptible flesh. This icon is a peaceful transmission, absolutely devoid of all emotional exaltation, of a certain spiritual reality. If grace enlightens the entire man, so that his entire spiritual and physical being is filled by prayer and exists in the divine light, the icon visibly captures this man who has become a living icon, a true likeness of God."[ii]

The icon's purpose is liturgical, it is an integral part of the liturgical expanse—the church building—and an ever-present participant in worship. Each icon, as a rule, reflects a particular church feast day, including saints' days.

The icon has a profound moral significance. Thus, for example, the image of the Holy Trinity, apart from symbolically pointing towards the triune Godhead, serves as a reminder of the spiritual unity towards which we are called by the Savior as members of Christ's one Church. The image of the Dormition of the Most Holy Theotokos conveys the historical event reflected in the feast day. At the same time, this image reveals that in Christianity death is perceived as a passage to everlasting life, where Christ awaits those who have believed in Him and obeyed His commandments.

Icons of Christ, the Theotokos, the Angels, and the Saints

Icons of Jesus Christ are of many different types. Thus, for example, on the icon of Christ Pantocrator, Jesus is portrayed as holding the Gospel. On the icon of the Savior Emmanuel, He is depicted as a young man with curly hair. On the icon of Christ in Majesty, He is seated on a throne surrounded by angels—the cherubim and the seraphim.

Christ Pantocrator.
15th c.

Christ Emmanuel.
End of 19th c.

Christ in Majesty.
Andrei Rublev. 1408.

Icons of the Theotokos are also of many different types, both with the Infant and without Him. The *Mother of God of Tenderness* is portrayed three-quarters turned towards the viewer, while the infant Christ has His cheek pressed up against her cheek. In the *Hodegetria* ("She who shows the Way") icon the Mother of God and the Infant are portrayed facing the viewer and the hand of the Infant is raised in a gesture of blessing. In the icon of the "Sign" the Theotokos is shown facing the viewer

Our Lady of the Don "Eleousa" (Tenderness)

Virgin Hodegetria (She Who Shows the Way)

Our Lady of the Sign

Virgin Mary from Deisis row

with the Infant in a circle (called a "mandorla"). The Theotokos is portrayed, particularly, without the Infant in those instances when her icon is part of the *Deisis* row.

Icons of the Mother of God, moreover, are distinguished from one another by their place of origin and veneration. We know of the Vladimir, Smolensk, Kostroma, Iviron, and many other such icons of the Theotokos. All of them have their own history and have been glorified by numerous miracles.

An angel is usually depicted on an icon in the form of a youth with wings. Some of the angelic ranks are shown in the iconographic tradition in a special manner: the cherubim with many eyes, and the seraphim with six wings.

The saints who have been canonized by the Church are also portrayed on icons. There are definite rules by

Angel. Miniature from the Khitrov Gospel. Andrei Rublev. Russia. End of 14th c.

Cherub. Detail of the icon "Sophia, the Wisdom of God." 1670s.

Saint Nicholas the Wonderworker

Saint Paraskeva

Saint Silouan the Athonite

Prophet Zechariah

which the saints are depicted. Thus, for example, the holy hierarchs are shown in their episcopal vestments, the martyrs holding a cross, the venerable monks in their monastic garb, and the prophets holding a scroll. Several saints can be depicted in one icon.

Some icons are called "**wonderworking**": these are icons through which miracles have happened, for example, numerous healings. Some icons are linked to victories in battle and deliverance from danger. Among the miraculous icons of the Mother of God, apart from those mentioned above, we can include the *Joy of All Who Sorrow*, the *Seeking of the Lost*, the *Unexpected Joy*, and many others. Icons of the Savior, the angels, and the saints can also be miraculous.

The Veneration of the Cross

The **veneration of the cross** occupies a special place in the Orthodox Church. Though it was once merely an instrument of punishment, it has become an instrument of redemption and a sign of victory over death. The cross is the main Christian symbol: it is venerated, people pray before it, and it is credited with miraculous power.

The veneration of the cross has a centuries-old theological basis. Already in the epistles of the Apostle Paul the cross is repeatedly mentioned. The apostle called the

Crosses on the dome of the Church of the Holy Sepulcher and on a street arch in Jerusalem.

preaching of the crucified Christ "foolishness to those who are perishing, but to us who are being saved it is the power of God" (1 Cor 1.18). Paul writes of himself: "But God forbid that I should boast except in the cross of our Lord Jesus Christ, by whom the world has been crucified to me, and I to the world." (Gal 6.14). The apostle speaks of how Christ reconciled us with God "through the cross, thereby putting to death the enmity" (Eph 2.16). In all these and many other instances when the apostle speaks of the cross in his epistles, the cross is a synonym for the crucifixion—the Savior's death on the cross.

The Orthodox Church dedicates a number of days of the year to the veneration of the cross: these are the week of the Veneration of the Cross (the third week of Lent), and the feast of the Exaltation of the Lord's Cross (September 14), as well as other feast days dedicated to the cross. Every Friday and on the days of Holy Week prayers are said to Christ's cross at services. Many prayers read in worship are addressed not only to Jesus crucified on the cross, but to the cross itself.[1]

The Orthodox Church has preserved the ancient custom of **crossing oneself** in worship and in domestic prayer. This custom is an integral part of holy Tradition.[iii] The faithful cross themselves in prayer as well as before beginning any undertaking. A priest's blessing is expressed in making the sign of the cross over the one who approaches him. The changing of the bread and wine into the Body and Blood of the Savior, the blessing of water in the sacrament of Baptism, and many other sacred actions are always performed by making the sign of the cross.

In the Orthodox tradition we encounter several types of depiction of the cross. The most widespread is the simple four-armed cross consisting of two beams: it is this type of cross that was most commonly used in the early Church. There is also the three-bar cross where the upper crossbeam symbolizes the sign with the inscription "Jesus of Nazareth, King of the Jews" and the lower beam symbolizes the footrest for the Savior. Sometimes this cross is shown on a calvary—a two-step pediment where to the viewer's left the spear is depicted, while to the right there is the reed with the sponge that was raised to Christ's lips. Apart from these symbolic images of the cross, we often find in churches a crucifix—an image of the Savior on the cross.

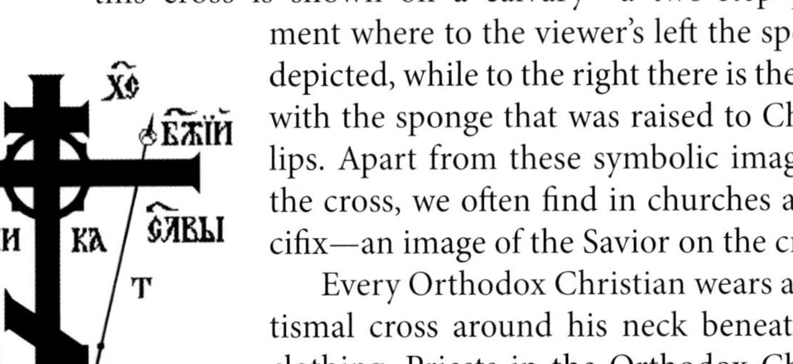

Every Orthodox Christian wears a baptismal cross around his neck beneath his clothing. Priests in the Orthodox Church wear a pectoral cross on top of their cassock.[2] At the services, along with the encolpion,[3] a bishop also wears a cross. Crosses are placed on the domes of church build-

[1] Addressing the cross in prayer is not the same as deifying the object, but a poetic form of glorifying the Savior, who shed His blood on the cross for the salvation of the world.

ings and chapels, and on the graves of Orthodox Christians. Crosses that are placed for veneration by the faithful in open places are called memorial crosses. These are erected in places of mass burials, in memory of deliverance from danger, in memory of the fact that a church once stood on this place, or as a sign that a church will be built there.

The veneration of the cross has remained for many centuries an integral part of the life of the Orthodox Church. It is inextricably linked to the veneration of the Lord and Savior crucified on the cross, and in liturgical texts the themes of the cross, the passion, the crucifixion, and the Resurrection are closely interwoven.

Christ's cross is the source of healing, it expels demons, and through it God's blessing is bestowed upon the faithful. The power that operates through the cross, however, is not an autonomous power peculiar to the cross: this power comes from the Lord Himself. And salvation, which flows from the cross, has as its cause not the cross in itself, but the fact that the Savior of the world, the Lord Jesus Christ, was crucified upon it.

Cross of Euphrosyne of Polotsk. 11th c.

[1] A cassock is the long black robe of a monk, priest, or bishop.

[2] An encolpion in Greek is Panagia meaning "All-Holy" and is a medallion with an image of the Mother of God. Sometimes the Savior or one of the saints can be depicted on the encolpion.

---

[i] Basil the Great, *On the Holy Spirit* 18.45 (Basil the Great, *On the Holy Spirit*, trans. Stephen Hildebrand, PPS 42 [Yonkers, NY: St Vladimir's Seminary Press, 2011], 81; cf. John of Damascus, *An Exact Exposition of the Orthodox Faith* 89; PPS 62:263; *Decree of the Seventh Ecumenical Council*, NPNF^2 14:550).

[ii] Leonid Ouspensky, *Theology of the Icon*, vol. 1, trans. Anthony Gythiel (Crestwood, NY: St Vladimir's Seminary Press, 1992), 166.

[iii] Basil the Great, *On the Holy Spirit* 27 (PPS 42:104).

6. Church Feast Days

The Church has a calendar that includes feasts and saints' days. It is based on the notion of the sanctification of time: every day of the church calendar is dedicated to the remembrance of a particular sacred event or holy person.

Feasts in the Church Calendar

The **church calendar** is structured in such a way that all the main events of the earthly life of Jesus Christ, through the cycle of the Lord's feasts throughout the year, pass by our spiritual gaze. In parallel we also touch upon the main events of the life of the Most Holy Theotokos in the feasts dedicated to her. Every day, moreover, particular saints are commemorated—both those of the early Church and those who lived in more recent times.

The feasts can either be **movable** or **fixed**. The fixed feasts are those that occur on the same date every year. The movable feasts are those that are celebrated on different days. The cycle of fixed feats is based upon the solar calendar, while that of the movable feasts depends upon the date of Pascha.

Some of the feasts are called "**Great**." They are, apart from Easter, the Twelve Great Feasts:

---

1. The Nativity of the Theotokos (September 8)
2. The Exaltation of the Cross (September 14)
3. The Entry of the Theotokos into the Temple (November 21)
4. The Nativity of Christ (Christmas) (December 25)
5. The Baptism of Christ in the Jordan (Theophany or Epiphany) (January 6)
6. The Meeting of Our Lord (The Presentation of Christ in the Temple) (February 2)

1

2

3

4

5

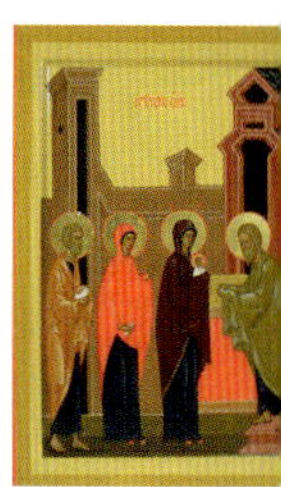
6

7. The Annunciation of the Theotokos (March 25)
8. The Entry of Our Lord into Jerusalem (Palm Sunday)
9. The Ascension of Our Lord Jesus Christ
10. Pentecost
11. The Transfiguration of Christ (August 6)
12. The Dormition of the Theotokos (August 15)

The Movable Feasts

Resurrection of Christ. Modern icon. Russia.

The main movable feast of the ecclesiastical year is the **Resurrection of Christ**. To commemorate the fact that the Savior's Resurrection occurred during the days of the celebration of the Jewish Passover, in Christian tradition this feast is also called the Passover, or Pascha. The word "Pascha" literally means "passing over." The event, however, in whose honor the ancient feast was established (the exodus of the people of Israel from Egyptian captivity), was reinterpreted in the Christian tradition as the prototype of Christ's Resurrection, thanks to which those who believe in Christ—the New Israel—make the transition from death to life, from time to eternity, from earth to heaven.

The date of the celebration of Pascha, or Easter, is calculated on a principle formulated in the fourth century: the first Sunday after the first full moon after the Spring equinox is chosen as the date for Easter. Easter may fall

8

9

10

11

12

on any of the thirty-five days between the 4th of April and the 8th of May according to the new calendar.[1]

The beginning of Lent depends upon the date of Pascha. It begins seven weeks before Pascha and concludes on the eve of Lazarus Saturday when we commemorate the raising of Lazarus (Jn 11.1–45). Then the feast of the **Entry of our Lord into Jerusalem** is celebrated a week before Pascha: it is dedicated to the triumphant entry of Jesus Christ into Jerusalem before His death on the cross.

Then **Holy Week** follows, when each day we commemorate the last days and hours of the earthly life of Jesus Christ (from Monday to Thursday), His death on the cross (Great and Holy Friday), and burial (Great and Holy Saturday). During the service for Holy Saturday the transition is made from the mourning of Holy Week to the Paschal rejoicing of Christ's Resurrection.

The date of Pascha also determines the dates of the feast of the **Ascension of our Lord** into heaven (on the fortieth day after Pascha) and **Pentecost** (on the fiftieth day after Easter), which is dedicated to the descent of the Holy Spirit upon the apostles.

[1] Or between March 22 and April 25 according to the old calendar; i.e., in parishes that use the Julian calendar, the celebration will take place thirteen days later on the civil calendar.

The Fixed Feasts

The main fixed feast of the ecclesiastical year is the **Nativity of Christ**. It is dedicated to the commemoration of the coming into the world of the Lord Jesus Christ through His birth from the Virgin Mary.

Eight days after the Nativity we celebrate the **Circumcision of the Lord** in Bethlehem (Lk 2.21).

On January 6 we celebrate the **Lord's Baptism** by St John the Baptist in the Jordan, and the revelation of the Trinity, for when Jesus came up out of the river, the heavens were opened, the Spirit, in the form of a dove, descended on Him, and the voice of Father said, "This is My beloved Son, in whom I am well pleased" (Mt 13.17). This feast is also known as Theophany or Epiphany.

Forty days after Nativity, the **Meeting of the Lord** is celebrated, when we recall how the Infant Jesus was brought into the Temple in Jerusalem. The Meeting in the Temple is considered to be both a Lord's feast and a feast of the Theotokos.

The feast of the **Annunciation of the Most Holy Theotokos** is celebrated nine months before Christ's Nativity. It is dedicated to the appearance of the archangel Gabriel to the Holy Virgin, when he announced that she would give birth to Christ (Lk 1.26–38).

The feast of the **Transfiguration of the Lord** is dedicated to an event described in three of the Gospels, when Jesus was transfigured before the disciples and His face shone like the sun.[2]

Among the feasts of the Theotokos, apart from the Annunciation and the Meeting in the Temple, we celebrate her **Nativity**, her **Presentation in the Temple**, and her **Dormition**.

The feast of the **Protection**, or, more fully, of the Protecting Veil of the Theotokos (October 1) belongs to the Great Feasts, but is not listed among the Twelve Feasts. It is dedicated to the appearance of the Mother of God

[2] The event was mentioned on page 35.

Protection of the Theotokos. Icon. Russia. 1399.

in the Church at Blachernae in Constantinople. The Holy Fool Andrew witnessed this appearance and then related it to the people gathered for worship.

As the ecclesiastical year begins in September and ends in August, the feast of the Nativity of the Theotokos is the first great feast of the year and the Dormition is the last.

Among the twelve feasts, apart from those mentioned above, is the **Exaltation of the Lord's Cross**: this feast was established to commemorate the discovery of the Lord's cross by the Empress Helena in the fourth century.

The saints' days are all the days of the ecclesiastical year, apart from the fixed great feasts of the Lord. The commemoration of some especially venerated saints, for example, St Nicholas the Wonderworker (December 6 and May 9) is celebrated with particular solemnity on a church-wide level. Moreover, in a particular country, region, diocese, and even parish there may be specially venerated saints.

If a church is dedicated to a particular saint, then this saint's day is called the "**patronal feast**" or "altar feast" of that church. If the church is named for a feast (e.g., the Transfiguration of the Lord), then this feast is also the "altar feast" of the church. If in the same church there are several side-chapels with altars dedicated to various saints or feasts, then this particular church has several "altar feasts."

Church feasts are different from secular holidays in that they are not an occasion for excessive drinking and eating, but rather a cause for spiritual joy. This is expressed in the way that the faithful go to church on that day and are united with Christ through the sacrament of Communion. At the same time, if fasting presupposes adherence to certain limitations in food, then the feasts usually allow us to set aside these limitations.

Fasts

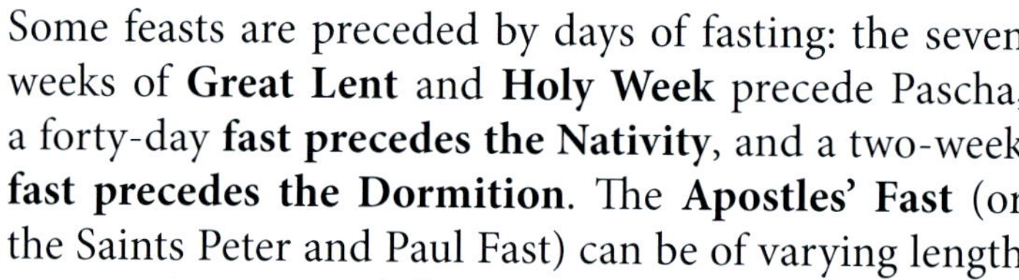

Some feasts are preceded by days of fasting: the seven weeks of **Great Lent** and **Holy Week** precede Pascha, a forty-day **fast precedes the Nativity**, and a two-week **fast precedes the Dormition**. The **Apostles' Fast** (or the Saints Peter and Paul Fast) can be of varying length in different years: it begins one week after the feast of Pentecost (whose date depends on the date of Pascha) and ends on the day of Saints Peter and Paul (June 29).

Apostles Peter and Paul. Icon. Byzantium. 14th c.

Apart from fasts lasting many days, there are also one-day fasts: these are Wednesday and Friday throughout the year,[3] as well as the feasts of the **Exaltation of the Lord's Cross** and the **Beheading of St John the Baptist** (August 29/September 11).

Fasts can vary in strictness: during strict fasts the church rules prescribe only vegetable foods without wine or oil, while on some days wine and oil or wine, oil, and fish are allowed.

A fast may be relaxed with the blessing of a priest for those who suffer from various illnesses, as well as for pregnant women and—with worthy cause—for other people.

[1] With the exception of the four "non-fasting" weeks when fasting on Wednesdays and Fridays is suspended (after Nativity, Pascha, Pentecost, and three weeks before Great Lent begins).

7. The Weekly and Daily Cycle of Services

Apart from the annual liturgical cycle, which includes the church feasts, there are also the weekly and daily cycles of services.

The Weekly Cycle of Worship

The **weekly cycle** is the seven days of worship, each of which is dedicated to a special theme. Sunday worship is dedicated to the commemoration of Christ's Resurrection. Sunday is considered to be the first and main day of the liturgical week: it is always a feast day. On Monday the Church commemorates the holy angels, on Tuesday St John the Baptist, on Wednesday and Friday Christ's crucifixion (it is for this reason that they are days of fasting, for it was on Wednesday that Judas betrayed Jesus and on Friday that the Savior was crucified), on Thursday the apostles and St Nicholas, and on Saturday all the departed.

The Daily Cycle of Worship

The **daily cycle** of worship consists of the church services that are celebrated throughout the course of the day: Vespers, Compline, the Midnight Office, Matins, the Hours (the First, Third, Sixth, and Ninth Hours) and the Liturgy (and sometimes the Typika). Vespers and Matins on the eve of Sunday are combined into a single service called the "**All-night Vigil**." In the early Church the All-night Vigil literally lasted all night, but in modern practice is begins and concludes in the evening. The First Hour is usually joined to the end of Matins, the Third and Sixth Hours are read before the Liturgy,

Worship in the Orthodox Church

Through worship a Christian enters into mysterious communion with his Creator through the sanctification of time and the performance of the sacraments, of which the main one is the sacrament of the Eucharist. The services are divided into three cycles: **daily, weekly, and annual**. The sacraments stand apart; they go beyond the time of this world.

1. Daily Cycle

All-night Vigil
A special evening service on the eve of major feasts and Sundays. Consists of Vespers, Matins and the First Hour.
Time: typically starts around 5:00 p.m.

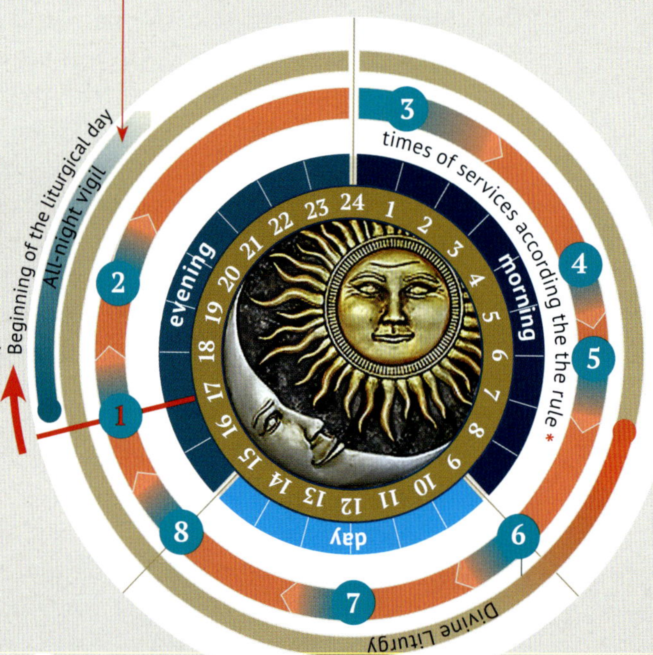

1 Vespers
Time: evening.
Purpose: thanksgiving for the passing day
Types: daily, great, small.

2 Compline
Time: after supper.
Purpose: prayer for forgiveness of sins, prayer before bed.
Types: great, small.

3 Midnight office
Time: between midnight and morning.
Purpose: remembrance of Christ's prayer in the Garden of Gethsemane, reminder of the Last Judgment.
Types: daily, Saturday, Sunday, Paschal.

4 Orthros
Time: morning.
Purpose: thanksgiving to God for past night and prayers for a new day.
Types: daily, feastal, Paschal.

5 First Hour *
Time: 6:00 a.m.
Purpose: a prayer for the coming day, a remembrance of the expulsion of Adam from paradise, and the appearance of Christ at the trial of Caiaphas.
Types: daily, Lenten, Royal, Paschal.

* *This way of reckoning time goes back to the ancient division of the day. Today, the Hours are usually joined to other services: the First Hour to Matins, the Third and Sixth to the Liturgy.*

6 Third Hour
Time: 9 a.m.
Purpose: commemoration of the descent of the Holy Spirit on the apostles.
Types: daily, Lenten, Royal, Paschal.

7 Sixth Hour
Time: noon.
Purpose: remembrance of Christ's crucifixion
Types: daily, Lenten, Royal, Paschal.

8 Ninth Hour
Time: 3 p.m.
Purpose: commemoration of Christ's death on the cross.
Types: daily, Lenten, Royal, Paschal.

Divine Liturgy

The Liturgy is timeless, it is not tied to the daily cycle and can be performed both in the morning and (in special cases) in the evening.
Time: can start in different ways, usually the start time varies from 7:00 a.m. to 10:00 p.m. (but on Mt Athos and in some monasteries it is served in the middle of the night).
Purpose: sacrament of the Eucharist.
Types: Liturgy of St John Chrysostom, of St Basil the Great, of the Presanctified Gifts.

2. Weekly Cycle

Each day of the week is dedicated to an event in sacred history or a saint.

1. Sunday
Resurrection of Christ

2. Monday
Angels

3. Tuesday
St John the Baptist

4. Wednesday
Betrayal of Judas, fast

5. Thursday
Apostles and St Nicholas

6. Friday
Suffering on the cross and death of the Savior, fast

7. Saturday
Holy Mother of God, all saints, remembrance of the dead

3. Yearly Cycle

Each day of the church year is dedicated to the memory of saints or holidays.

1. Fixed annual circle of worship

• The beginning of the church year (indication) is September 1.
• The fixed annual circle includes "immovable" (or fixed) feast days tied to a specific date.
• Some Orthodox Churches use the Julian calendar, the so-called "old style."
• Today, its "lag" relative to the Gregorian is 13 days.

2. Movable annual circle of services

• Associated with the celebration of Pascha. Orthodox Pascha is celebrated between April 4 and May 8.
• The moving annual circle includes the services of Lent (and the three preceding weeks), Pascha and the time before Pentecost, and the day of Pentecost itself.

while the Ninth Hour precedes Vespers. Typika is a service used on days when the Liturgy is not celebrated. It consists of selected elements from the Liturgy, without the Anaphora. It is ordinarily done in liturgical recitative. It is served most often in monasteries, but in parish churches when no priest is available, this service may be served by the laity in a more solemn form, with melody. The lenten weekday form of this office is slightly different, and then it usually follows the Ninth Hour.

At all church services psalms from the Old Testament Psalter are recited. The **Psalter** contains 150 psalms and is prescribed to be read in its entirety in the church services weekly (during Lent it is read twice a week). The backbone of Vespers, Matins, and the Hours is made up of psalms specially selected for these services. In addition, at these services hymns are sung, which were composed by Christian authors (mainly from the first millennium) dedicated to the Church's feasts and various saints' days.

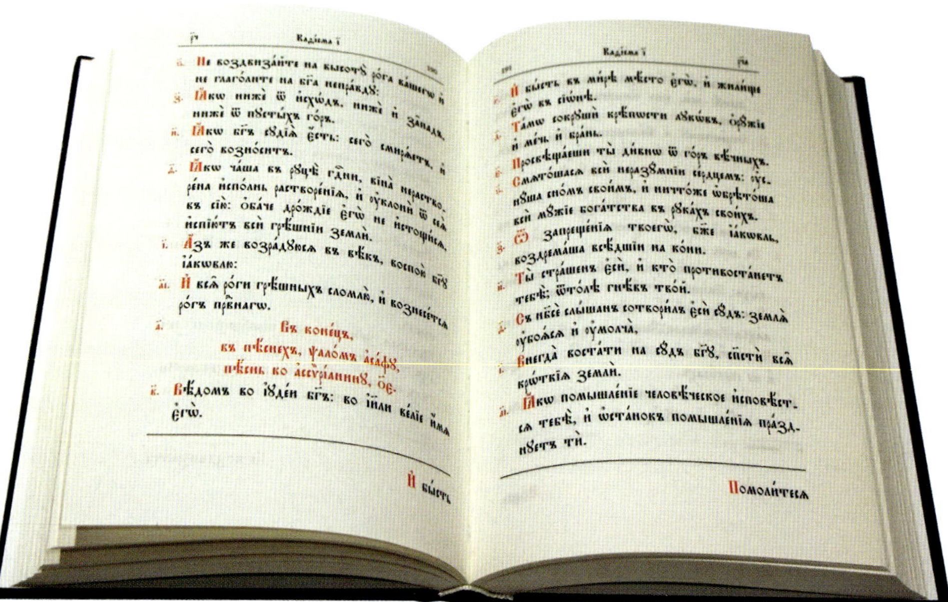

The Distinguishing Features of Orthodox Worship

All the elements of Orthodox divine worship—architecture, icons and frescos, church vessels, reading and singing, solemn processions, and the ringing of bells—are not intended to distract the attention of the faithful, but on the contrary to dispose them towards prayer, towards the praise of God, in which, according to the teaching of the Church, not only does the Church on earth participate, but also the Church in heaven; not only human beings, but the angels.

The human person participates in worship using all of the senses: mainly hearing and sight, but also touch (through venerating the icons and holy objects), smell (during the censing of the church with sweet-smelling incense), and taste (through the Communion of consecrated Bread and Wine and by drinking holy water).[1]

A notable characteristic of Orthodox divine worship is its **length**. One after another, without pause, there follow psalms, the prayerful petitions of the deacon, the singing of the choir, the prayers and the exclamations of the priest: the entire service is experienced in a single breath as a ceaseless unfolding mystery. The Byzantine liturgical texts, replete with deep theological content, are interspersed with psalms originally written in ancient Hebrew, with readings from Scripture, and with the words of the priests on the topics of these readings (the sermon).

Worship in most churches of the Russian tradition is conducted in the Church Slavonic language. In many countries worship is conducted in the **national languages**, for example, in English in America and Great Britain, in Japanese in Japan, and so on.

[1] The inability of a particular bodily organ to function is, however, not an obstacle to participating in worship. At present special orders of service have been compiled for the those with hearing or visual disabilities.

8. The Eucharist

The main service of the daily cycle is the **Divine Liturgy** at which the main sacrament of the Church is celebrated: the **Eucharist**.

The Greek word *leitourgia* literally means "common work" (or "work of the people")—since ancient times this word has been used to denote the service at which the breaking of bread was performed in remembrance of the Last Supper.

The word "Eucharist" means "thanksgiving," which is the basic prayerful disposition of the priest and the people at this service.

8.1. The Eucharist as the Foundation of the Life of the Church

The Eucharist is the Church's most important sacrament. It is known as the "sacrament of sacraments," as it is the heart of church life, the foundation upon which the whole body of the Church is built. Without participation in the Eucharist, we cannot be saved, nor can we enter into everlasting life.

The Lord Jesus Christ spoke about this: "I am the bread of life. … I am the living bread which came down from heaven. … If anyone eats of this bread, he will live forever; and the bread that I shall give is My flesh, which I shall give for the life of the world. … Most assuredly, I say to you, unless you eat the flesh of the Son of Man and drink His blood, you have no life in you. Whoever eats My flesh and drinks My blood has eternal life, and I will raise him up on the last day. For My flesh is food indeed and My blood is drink indeed. He who eats My flesh and drinks My blood abides in Me, and I in him" (Jn 6.48–56).

Last Supper. Icon. Athos, Greece. 1976.

The Eucharist is the renewal and continuation of the Last Supper—the last meal of Jesus with the disciples, when He gave them His Body and Blood under the guise of bread and wine.

After the Savior's Resurrection, His disciples would gather on the first day of the week (Sunday) in order to break bread in remembrance of Him. The eucharistic meal began in the evening and could last until the morning (Acts 20.7–11). The meal bore a solemn and liturgical nature, its basic tone was that of thanksgiving. At the meal there were readings from the Old Testament, lengthy teachings were read aloud (Acts 20.9, 11), and "psalms, hymns, and spiritual songs" were sung (Col 3.16). The Eucharist itself—the act of the breaking of bread in remembrance of Jesus Christ—was celebrated at the end of the meal.

In time, the Eucharist was transformed from a meal into an act of worship celebrated according to a clearly established liturgical order. But the nature of the meal was retained in the sacrament of the Eucharist by the act of Holy Communion.

The Church believes that each time the Eucharist is celebrated, Christ stands at its head. It is He who is the true celebrant of the Eucharist, operating through the priest or bishop who heads the eucharistic assembly.

All of the church community takes part in the Eucharist. The Eucharist is not a sacred action performed by the priest for the people: it is the bloodless sacrifice that all of the community—with the priest at the head—offers up to God.

The Bread and the Wine in the Eucharist

What happens to the bread and wine at the Eucharist? At the prayers of the priest and the church community, the Holy Spirit comes down upon them, and they **become the Body and Blood of Christ**.

It has been the belief of the Church from the very beginning that the eucharistic bread and wine become the real, and not symbolic, Body and Blood of Christ after their **transformation**. This belief is preserved in the Orthodox Church. After their transformation, the bread and wine retain their outward appearance and physical properties, but in their substance they become the Body and Blood of the Savior. They are called the Holy Mysteries or Holy Gifts, emphasizing that this is the most important sacred object of the Church, God's precious and mysterious gift to people.

Union with God through Holy Communion

At the Last Supper Jesus said to His disciples: "I am the vine, you are the branches" (Jn 15.5). Through faith in Jesus Christ as God and Savior, through Communion with His flesh and blood and participation in the life of the Church and by fulfilling His commandments, we may be united with Christ in a special, supernatural way. We can be grafted onto Christ like a branch to the vine and can be sustained by Him through the life-giving sap that restores to life branches that have dried up and died (see Jn 15.1–8).

In receiving Holy Communion, a Christian receives God within himself. The entry of the Body and Blood of the Son of God into our body and blood signifies our perfect and complete union with God. This union is impossible to attain by any other means. Through prayer we can communicate with God, open up our hearts to Him, and listen to His response. Through good deeds we can please God and call down His beneficent will upon us. But it is only through Holy Communion that we are united with God spiritually and physically, that we receive Him within ourselves so that our body is united with His Body, and His Blood flows in our veins.

The Holy Fathers taught that through Communion the faithful become the **kinsmen of God**, they are united to Him into a single flesh. In assuming flesh, the Son of God became our brother, and we become His brothers in Communion by becoming a part of His Godhead through His flesh: "He has become our kinsman in the flesh, and has rendered us co-participants in his divinity, and so has made us all his kinsmen," writes St Symeon the New Theologian (tenth–eleventh c.). "Just as Eve was taken from the flesh and bones of Adam and the two were one flesh, so also Christ gives himself to us to the extent of Communion of His flesh."[i]

Elsewhere the same saint writes: "You are our kinsman by the flesh, while we are Your kinsmen according to Your Divinity. … In being united, we all become a single dwelling-place, that is, all of us become Your relatives, all of us are Your brothers. … You abided with us now and for all the ages, and make of each one of us an abode and You live in all of us … each of us separately with You, O Savior, all with You who are All, and You are with each of us separately, the One with the one. … In this manner all of the members of each of us are made members of Christ. … And we together are made gods, abiding with God."[ii]

The Holy Fathers call "**deification**" the new quality of being that the human person acquires at the heights

His Beatitude, Metropolitan Tikhon preparing the Holy Eucharist.

of holiness through the operation of divine grace; that is, the state when the human person, in uniting with God, acquires divine qualities. One of the effectual means of attaining this state is Holy Communion. Through Communion, God, who abides in the heavens, does not merely come down from heaven to earth, but He takes up His abode in our body and heart, lives in us, sanctifying and illumining us inwardly, transforming our human nature and filling it with his life-giving presence.

St John Chrysostom (fourth century) writes the following about the Blood of Christ, which the faithful receive: "This blood causes the image of our king to be fresh within us, produces an unspeakable beauty, stops the nobleness of our souls from wasting away, watering it continually, and nourishing it. … This blood, if rightly taken, drives away devils, and keeps them afar off from us, while it calls to us angels and the Lord of angels. For wherever they see the Lord's blood, devils flee, and angels run together. This blood, which has been shed, washed clean all the world. … This blood is the salvation of our souls, by this the soul is washed, by this it is made beautiful, by this it is set aflame, this blood causes our understanding to be more bright than fire, and our soul more beaming than gold; this blood was poured forth, and made heaven accessible."[iii]

Preparation for Communion

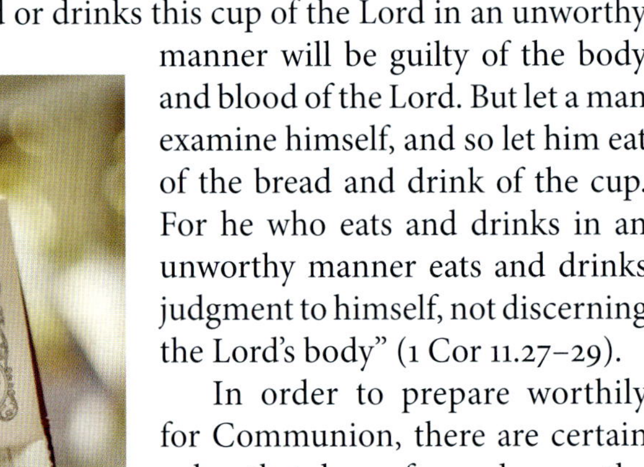

It is important to **prepare** for Holy Communion. The Apostle Paul reminds us of this: "Therefore whoever eats this bread or drinks this cup of the Lord in an unworthy manner will be guilty of the body and blood of the Lord. But let a man examine himself, and so let him eat of the bread and drink of the cup. For he who eats and drinks in an unworthy manner eats and drinks judgment to himself, not discerning the Lord's body" (1 Cor 11.27–29).

In order to prepare worthily for Communion, there are certain rules that have formed over the centuries. First, on the morning before Communion we should not eat or drink. Moreover, before Communion it is customary to go to Confession in order to cleanse our soul from sins and receive forgiveness from God (there are different local traditions regarding how often believers should confess or how recent confession must be before receiving Communion). The faithful are invited on the eve of the Liturgy at which they will receive Com-

munion to attend the evening service and at home to read *The Office for Preparation for Holy Communion*—a series of prayers from the *Orthodox Prayer Book*. Many Christians observe a fast for one or several days before receiving Communion.

These rules may be relaxed with a priest's blessing or even dropped altogether in special cases, for example, during grave illness. The formalistic attitude to the religious life, which was characteristic of the Pharisees, is alien to the Christian Church: "Observe a certain number of rules, and you will be pleasing to God." The most important element in preparing for Communion is to recall that God looks at the heart of the human person and its inward disposition: He awaits our love for Him and not a mechanical observance of particular rules. "My son, give Me your heart, and let your eyes observe My ways," says biblical Wisdom (Prov 23.26), which personifies God. The existing practice of preparing for Communion is not an end in itself: it is aimed at helping us to acquire the right disposition, to cleanse our souls and hearts for the worthy reception of the Body and Blood of Christ.

How Often Should We Receive Communion?

In the early Church, the faithful received Communion at every Eucharist: the notion that a baptized Christian could attend the Liturgy and stand through it while not receiving Communion was completely absent. At certain times and in some countries the practice arose of infrequent Communion, most often as a result of strict rules of preparation. At present many of the faithful receive Communion every Sunday and on all of the great feast days. Individual preparation for the sacrament may be discussed with one's spiritual father[1] or parish priest.

8.2. The Order of Celebrating the Divine Liturgy

There are three types of Divine Liturgy used in the Orthodox Church: of St Basil the Great, of St John Chrysostom, and of the Presanctified Gifts. The **Liturgy of St Basil the Great** is celebrated ten times a year: on the eve of the feasts of Nativity (Christmas) and Theophany (or Epiphany), the day of St Basil the Great, on Sundays during Lent, on Holy Thursday, and on Holy Saturday. On the remaining days of the year, with the exception of weekdays of Lent, the **Liturgy of St John Chryso-**

[1] A spiritual father is the priest to whom an Orthodox Christian regularly makes his Confession and to whom he turns when necessary for advice. Every Christian, whenever possible, ought to have a spiritual father.

stom is celebrated. On Wednesdays and Fridays of Lent the **Liturgy of the Presanctified Gifts** is celebrated. On Mondays, Tuesdays, and Thursdays of Lent the Liturgy is customarily not celebrated at all.

The Liturgies of Basil the Great and John Chrysostom differ only in the length and content of the prayers that the priest reads before the altar. In some places, these prayers are not read aloud, and thus the difference between these two Liturgies is not noticeable to the congregation. The distinguishing feature of the Liturgy of the Presanctified Gifts is that the sacrament of the Eucharist is not celebrated at it (that is, the transformation of the bread and wine does not take place); rather the faithful receive Communion from the Holy Gifts that were prepared and "presanctified" at the previous complete Liturgy when the Eucharist was celebrated.

Divine Liturgy (further we will speak only about Liturgies of Saint Basil the Great and Saint John Chrysostom) begins with **proskomedia** (Greek "offering"), performed by the priest in the altar. The preparation of the bread and wine for the Eucharist takes place, accompanied by special prayers.

The Liturgy itself is divided into two parts: the Liturgy of the Catechumens and the Liturgy of the Faithful. In the early Church the catechumens—that is, those who were being catechized and were preparing to receive Baptism—were permitted to attend the first part of the Liturgy. They were to leave the church at the exclamation: "All catechumens, depart!" after which only the faithful (the baptized) remained in church, who would then participate in the sacrament of the Eucharist and receive Holy Communion.

The Liturgy of the Catechumens

The **Liturgy of the Catechumens** (sometimes called the "Liturgy of the Word") has a primarily didactic nature. It begins with the exclamation: "Blessed is the kingdom

Divine Liturgy

Liturgy (Greek: "work of the people") is the main worship service of the Church. At the Liturgy, the sacrament of the Eucharist is celebrated: under the guise of bread and wine, believers partake of the body and blood of Christ.

There are several rites of the Liturgy. They differ in the supposed authorship of the main part of the service—the Liturgy of the Faithful and the Anaphora itself (Greek for "offering")—during which the bread and wine mysteriously become the body and blood of the Savior.

Main rites of the Orthodox Liturgy

1. The Divine Liturgy of Saint John Chrysostom

Compiler of rites: Saint John Chrysostom.
Served: throughout the year, unless the canon prescribes otherwise.

2. The Divine Liturgy of Saint Basil the Great

Compiler of rites: Saint Basil the Great.
Served: ten times a year: on the eves of Christmas and Theophany or on these feasts themselves if they fall on Sunday or Monday; on the feast day of St Basil the Great; on the first, second, third, fourth, and fifth Sundays of Lent, on Holy Thursday and Holy Saturday.
Special feature: the prayers that the priest reads at the altar are longer compared to the prayers of the Liturgy of John Chrysostom. Therefore the choir sings in a slow and drawn out manner.

3. Liturgy of the Presanctified Gifts

Compiler of rites: Gregory the Dialogist
Served: on Wednesdays and Fridays of Lent, as well as on feast days of especially revered saints that fall on weekdays of Lent.
Special feature: there is no consecration of the eucharistic gifts at the Presanctified Liturgy. Holy Communion is given from the eucharistic gifts sanctified on the previous Sunday at the celebration of the Divine Liturgy.

Bishop's book-bearer →

of the Father, and of the Son, and of the Holy Spirit, now and ever, and unto ages of ages." Then the Great Litany follows—a series of petitions for peace, for the Church, for the civil and church authorities, for the church building and those who enter therein with faith and reverence, for seasonable weather, and so that God's grace help the faithful and preserve them. Then we sing Psalms 102 and 145 and the hymn *Only-begotten Son and Word of God*, in which the Church turns to Jesus Christ as the Word of God, who became man "for our salvation."

After the singing of the Trisagion—"Holy God, Holy Mighty, Holy Immortal, have mercy on us"—two readings follow, one from the Acts of the Apostles, the Catholic Epistles, or the Epistles of St Paul; and the other from the Gospel. Then a series of litanies follows—a series of prayerful petitions with prayers read by the priest in the sanctuary. The Liturgy of the Catechumens concludes with the exclamation: "Catechumens, depart!"

The Liturgy of the Faithful

The **Liturgy of the Faithful** then begins without any pause. The Great Entrance is made, during which the Holy Gifts—the bread and wine prepared for the Eucharist—are brought from the table of oblation into the nave and through the holy doors into the sanctuary, where they are placed on the holy table.

During the Great Entrance, the Cherubic Hymn is sung: "Let us who mystically represent the cherubim and who sing the Thrice-Holy hymn to the Life-giving Trinity, now lay aside all earthly cares, that we may receive the King of all, who comes invisibly upborne by the angelic hosts. Alleluia."[2] The text of the Cherubic Hymn reflects the Church's belief that not only people on earth, but also the angels, participate in divine worship.

[2] The Hebrew word Alleluia means "praise the Lord." This word, like the word Amen ("truly") entered Christian liturgical usage without translation.

Liturgy in an Orthodox church in Cuba.

After the Great Entrance, more petitions follow, after which the Creed is sung or read. The solemn proclamation of the Creed before the Eucharist testifies to the notion that from the Church's perspective the correct faith and confession of the basic dogmas of the Church is the essential condition for union with God.

The Anaphora or Eucharistic Canon

The main part of the Liturgy—the Eucharist—begins with the blessing based on the words of the Apostle Paul: "The grace of our Lord Jesus Christ, and the love of God the Father, and the communion of the Holy Spirit be with all of you" (cf. 2 Cor 13.13). After this blessing, the choir responds: "And with your spirit," and the priest repeats the ancient liturgical exclamations "Let us lift up our hearts" and "Let us give thanks unto the Lord."

The prayer of thanksgiving, called the **Anaphora** or **Eucharistic Canon**, is read by the priest in the sanctuary.[3] This prayer (significantly longer in the Liturgy of Basil the Great than in the Liturgy of John Chrysostom, but similar in content in both Liturgies) contains thanksgiving to God for the fact that He, invisible, unknown, and incomprehensible, created the world and man, that after the fall He did not turn away from him, but revealed Himself to people, sending to them the prophets and teachers; especially for the fact that "He gave His only begotten Son, that whoever who believes in Him should not perish but have everlasting life" (Jn 3.16). The basic events of the life and saving work of the Lord Jesus Christ are commemorated, from His birth, to His death on the cross, to His Resurrection from the dead, to His Ascension into heaven, to His second coming (thus the past and future are united in prayer). The Last Supper, at which Christ gave to His disciples His Body and Blood, is commemorated in a special way.

After this prayer, the priest then exclaims aloud the words uttered by Christ Himself at the Last Supper: "Take, eat, this is My body which is broken for you for the remission of sins"; "Drink of this all of you, this is My blood of the New Covenant, which is shed for you and for many for the remission of sins." After saying these words, the priest prays that the Holy Spirit may come down upon the faithful and upon the Holy Gifts, making them the Body and Blood of Christ. From this moment onwards it is not bread and wine on the altar but the **Body and Blood of the Savior**.

His Eminence, the Most Reverend Daniel, Archbishop of Chicago and the Midwest (Orthodox Church in America) during the Great Entrance. →

Then the preparation for Holy Communion begins, and after a series of prayers and hymns, the "Our Father" is read or sung. This has a special meaning before Communion, since it contains the words: "Give us this day our daily bread." In this instance, the words "daily bread" are understood as pointing not to ordi-

[3] In some places this prayer is read aloud, in other places silently.

IC XC
NI KA

nary food but to the bread that the Savior says, "comes down from heaven and gives life to the world" (Jn 6.33).

Holy Communion

The exclamation: "The holy things are for the holy," which can be heard before the clergy begin to take Communion in the sanctuary, signifies that the Holy Gifts are intended only for the "holy"—that is, for those who have believed in Christ and accepted Baptism. In the early Church, the term "the saints" (or "holy ones") was applied to *all* Christians; in our day it reminds us of the vocation to holiness that all Christians share.

After the clergy receive Holy Communion, the holy doors are opened and the chalice with the Body and Blood of Christ is brought out so that the faithful can receive Communion. The communicants approach the chalice with reverence and place their hands across their breast in the form of a cross; they say their names audibly and open their mouths so that the priest can place the spoon in them with a particle of the Body of Christ and a small amount of his Blood.[4] After this the communicant kisses the bottom of the chalice and withdraws in order to eat a piece of antidoron (blessed bread) so that the particle can be consumed properly.

The Liturgy concludes with solemn prayers of thanksgiving and hymns and the exclamation "Let us depart in peace" (which indicates that the communicant is to leave the church in a state of spiritual tranquility) and the accompanying blessing of the priest. At the end of the Liturgy, the faithful kiss the cross.

[4] At Communion one should not say anything other than one's name. It is wrong to thank the priest, ask questions, and so on. One should not move or attempt to "help" the priest by biting at the spoon with the particle on it. One ought to stand upright and still, open wide one's mouth and close it immediately after the spoon has been placed in the mouth. It is not appropriate to cross oneself either before or straight after Communion for fear of upsetting the chalice.

Holy Communion ↑

The Body and Blood of Christ are great and holy. They are to be treated carefully and with reverence. After Communion, we ought not to engage in the vanity of worldly affairs. It is important to preserve as long as possible the inner peace that is communicated to us by uniting with God. Ideally, the Christian should never lose this inner spiritual peace. He tries not to offend God's holiness by a bad or sinful act and recalls that God does not look upon him from the outside but—thanks to the sacrament of Holy Communion—lives within him.

---

[i] Symeon the New Theologian, *Ethical Discourse* 1.6; St Symeon the New Theologian, *On the Mystical Life: The Ethical Discourses*, vol. 1: *The Church and the Last Things*, trans. Alexander Golitzin, Popular Patristics Series 14 (Crestwood, NY: St Vladimir's Seminary Press, 1995), 45, 47.

[ii] Symeon the New Theologian, *Hymn* 15.121–154; SC 156:286–290; cf. *Divine Eros: Hymns of Saint Symeon the New Theologian*, trans. Daniel K. Griggs, Popular Patristics Series 40 (Crestwood, NY: St Vladimir's Seminary Press, 2010), 86–87.

[iii] John Chrysostom, *Homilies on the Gospel of John* 46.3; NPNF[1] 14:166–167 (language updated).

The Seven Sacraments

Sacrament—a sacred act through which the grace of God acts on a person. The sacraments were established by Christ or His apostles and are designed to change the inner life of a person.

1. Baptism

The Essence of the Sacrament:
Joining the Church, being born in Christ.

Main act:
Immersion in water three times while saying the words: "The servant of God (name) is baptized in the name of the Father. Amen. And the Son. Amen. And the Holy Spirit. Amen."

2. Chrismation

The Essence of the Sacrament:
Sanctification of the whole person, granting of the gift of the Holy Spirit.

Main act:
Cross-shaped anointing of the newly baptized with the consecrated chrism done by the priest over the forehead, eyes, nostrils, ears, chest, hands, and feet with the words "Seal of the gift of the Holy Spirit. Amen."

3. Holy Communion

The Essence of the Sacrament:
The union of the believer with Christ.

Main act:
At the Divine Liturgy celebration during the sacrament of the Eucharist bread and wine are transformed into the true Body and Blood of Christ, which the believers receive. The central point of the Liturgy is the recitation of the "anaphora" prayer with the blessing of bread and wine. From this prayer, believers in the church hear only the words spoken by Christ at the establishment of the Eucharist at the Last Supper: "Take, eat, this is My Body, broken for you for the remission of sins! Amen. Drink of it, all of you, this is My Blood, the New Covenant, which is shed for you and for many for the remission of sins! Amen" (see Mt. 26.26–28).

4. Confession

The Essence of the Sacrament:
Confession of sins to God and receiving forgiveness.

Main act:
After the penitent has named his sins, the priest, who is present at the celebration of the sacrament and is a witness of repentance, says two prayers. The first contains the words "reconcile and unite him with Your Holy Church." The second is called "absolution."

5. Holy Unction (Anointing of the Sick)

The Essence of the Sacrament:
Healing of spiritual and physical ailments by the grace of God.

Main act:
Readings of seven passages from the Epistles and the Gospel. After each reading, the priest says a prayer for the sick person and anoints his forehead, cheeks, chest and hands with consecrated oil. At the end of the reading, the priest places the opened Gospel on the head of the person being unctioned and prays for the forgiveness of his sins.

6. Holy Orders

The Essence of the Sacrament:
Through the laying on of hands by the bishop, the believer is given grace to serve and to perform the sacraments.

Main act:
Ordination takes place during the Liturgy. At the end of the rite, the newly ordained is dressed in vestments corresponding to his new rank, while the bishop (or council of bishops) performing the sacrament proclaims "Axios!" (Greek, "worthy"), to which the priests and choir respond with three times "Axios!", "worthy!"

7. Marriage

The Essence of the Sacrament:
Blessing marriage as a joint path to God.

Main act:
During the sacrament of Marriage, the priest places crowns on the heads of the bride and groom, pronouncing the petition three times: "Lord our God, crown them with glory and honor."

9. Other Sacraments and Rites

We spoke above of three sacraments: in the first part of the Catechism we spoke of Baptism and Chrismation, and in the previous chapter of the third part we spoke of the Eucharist. We must still speak of the four other sacraments, as well as other church rites.

9.1. Confession

Repentance, or Confession, is the sacrament during which the Christian names his sins, and the priest on behalf of God grants forgiveness for them.

Many people do not see their own sins and shortcomings. The inability to evaluate oneself critically (while at the same paying exaggerated attention to the faults of others) is an extremely common spiritual sickness. The Lord Jesus Christ spoke of it: "Why do you look at the speck in your brother's eye, but do not consider the plank in your own eye? Or how can you say to your brother, 'Let me remove the speck from your eye'; and look, a plank is in your own eye? Hypocrite! First remove the plank from your own eye, and then you will see clearly to remove the speck from your brother's eye" (Mt 7.3–5).

This sickness is healed by **repentance.** Repentance is not unjust self-condemnation or the scourging of oneself: it requires a sober, healthy, yet critical view of oneself. This view is difficult to acquire without God's aid. That is why in one of the prayers read during Lent we say: "Lord, grant me to see my own sins and not to condemn my brother."

The ability to see one's own sins and shortcomings is the most important prerequisite for repentance. In order to see one's sins, it is necessary to check one's life against the Gospel constantly—especially the Savior's Sermon on the Mount from the Gospel of Matthew (Mt 5.1–7.29) and His other teachings. In the light of these teachings, as in a mirror, we see everything that leaves us short of the moral ideal.

Confession can take the form of prayerful turning towards God or the form of a conversation with a priest. It is not the form but the content that is important in Confession. One ought not to talk in detail about sins that have been committed by going into the circumstances and various attendant factors. One ought not to speak of others' sins or complain about other people. One ought not to turn Confession into a discussion of "problems," life's difficulties, or theological issues. Confession is first and foremost telling one's own faults, sins, and vices. The condition for being freed from them and receiving forgiveness is the firm desire of the penitent to renounce them or at least to struggle against them.

People who come to Confession very often name the same sins. This does not mean that Confession is of no use. Liberation from sin does not happen automatically. Sins are nothing other than **spiritual sicknesses**. As in the case of bodily illnesses, it is very important to make the correct diagnosis: this diagnosis is made by the person himself at Confession, and the priest helps him in this. Further, it is no less important to describe the symptoms of the sickness of one's soul so that the doctor can select the correct spiritual cure. Healing, though, can be a lengthy and complex process lasting many years.

The closer one is to God, the greater one realizes one's sinfulness and imperfection, the more acutely one becomes aware of one's shortcomings. The Apostle Paul considered himself to be first among sinners (1 Tim 1.15). Repentance leads us towards a profound awareness of our sinfulness, while in others we begin to see fewer and fewer faults, and if we do see them, then we are able to separate the sin from the sinner, the sickness from the patient.

Repentance is the re-evaluation of values, a profound transformation of our views of our self and those around us. Genuine repentance does not lead to despondency or despair. It can, on the contrary, bring us deep inner joy, similar to that of someone who has recovered his health after a lengthy and grave illness.

Confession concludes with the priest reciting the prayer of absolution over the penitent in which God forgives him all his sins. The one condition for the effectiveness of this prayer is the sincerity of the penitent. If out of a false sense of shame or other consideration we come to Confession and conceal particular sins from the priest, then we do not receive forgiveness from God, and spiritual healing does not take place.

9.2. Marriage

Marriage, or crowning, is the sacred action performed over people who want to enter a marital union. The Church teaches that "matrimony is a sacrament, in which, on the free promise of the man and woman before the priest and the Church to be true to each other, their conjugal union is blessed to be an image of Christ's union with the Church, and grace is asked for them to live together in godly love and honesty, to the procreation and Christian bringing up of children."[i]

In accordance with the early ecclesiastical canons, only those who confess the Orthodox faith are admitted to the sacrament of Matrimony.[1]

The sacrament of Marriage consists of two parts: the betrothal and the crowning. The betrothal can be done separately from the crowning or immediately before it. At the betrothal the future spouses declare an oath of fidelity to each other and the priest reads a prayer in which God blesses their marital union.

The structure of the rite of crowning is reminiscent of the Divine Liturgy: this is so because in the early Church the crowning was often performed at the Liturgy and the entire church community would attend the sacrament (in modern practice the crowning is often performed apart from the Liturgy; local customs vary). The rite of crowning involves the placing of crowns upon the heads of the bride and the groom, as well as various prayers that reveal the meaning of the marital union.

This meaning is also revealed through the reading of a passage from the Apostle Paul's Epistle to the Ephesians: "Wives, submit to your own husbands, as to the Lord. For the husband is head of the wife, as also Christ is head of the church; and He is the Savior of the body. Therefore, just as the Church is subject to Christ, so let the wives be to their own husbands in everything. Husbands, love your wives, just as Christ also loved the Church and gave Himself for her. … So husbands ought to love their own wives as their own bodies; he who loves his wife loves himself. … This is a great mystery, but I speak concern-

[1] At the same time, *The Basis of the Social Concept of the Russian Orthodox Church* (10.2) states: "Proceeding from considerations of pastoral *oikonomia*, the Russian Orthodox Church has deemed it possible, both in the past and present, to celebrate marriages between Orthodox Christians and Catholics, members of the Oriental Churches, and Protestants who confess the faith in the Triune God, provided the marriage is blessed in the Orthodox Church and the children are raised in the Orthodox faith." Regarding marriages between Orthodox and non-Christians, the same document states that the Church does not sanctify their marriage, "while recognising them as lawful and not regarding those who live in such a marriage as living in sinful co-habitation."

The Sacrament of Marriage

Marriage is one of the seven sacraments of the Orthodox Church. The first marriage took place in heaven, so the purpose of the wedding is to unite a man and a woman for the sake of returning to the original state of happiness, including through the birth of children.

In the early Church, marriage was celebrated through the joint participation of the bride and groom in the Eucharist. According to the rules of the Orthodox Church, weddings are not celebrated in fasting seasons, nor on the eves of Wednesdays, Fridays, Sundays, and great feasts. A church wedding takes place only after a conversation with a priest and registration at the registry office.

3. Crowns

The very name of the sacrament comes from the word "crowns"—images of divine glory, which are awarded to pious spouses who humbly endure the difficulties of living together. Marriage is usually called the royal path to the salvation of the soul.

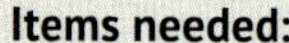

Items needed:

1. Wedding rings

The betrothal with rings takes place immediately before the wedding in the narthex of the temple. The rings are blessed on the altar table, and the exchange of rings occurs as a sign of divine blessing and firm agreement to follow the chosen path.

4. Common cup

In remembrance of the Gospel miracle of turning water into wine (Jn 2.1–11), the spouses partake of wine from a common cup, which symbolizes their unity for the sake of procreation and is a blessing for the joy that living together gives.

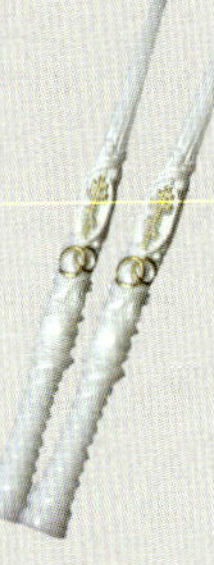

2. Wedding candles

Melting candles are symbols of human life, fleeting, but called upon to burn with bright faith and fiery love. It is customary to keep for life these two wedding candles, representing two souls ready for eternity.

5. Icons of Christ and Theotokos

After the sacrament is performed, the spouses are often presented with icons of Christ and the Mother of God as images of love by which the whole world was redeemed and which they must keep and protect throughout their lives.

Christ and the Virgin Mary at the wedding feast in Cana of Galilee. Fresco. Dionysius. Russia. 15th c.

ing Christ and the Church. Nevertheless let each one of you in particular so love his own wife as himself, and let the wife see that she respects her husband" (Eph 5.22–33).

We ought not to see in these words merely a reflection of the ancient patriarchal order, according to which the husband was the head of the family, and the wife occupied a position of submission. The accent is primarily on **marital fidelity:** the husband's love of his wife is to be sacrificial; he is to care for her and love her according to the image of the sacrificial and self-sacrificing love of Christ for the Church, while the wife is to strive never to offend her husband in anything.

Then the priest reads the Gospel narrative of the wedding feast in Cana of Galilee, at which Jesus Christ turned water into wine (Jn 2.1–11). The reading of this Gospel emphasizes the sacramental nature of marriage. In the sacraments, material objects are filled with the divine presence, acquiring healing properties through their transformation by the operation of the Holy Spirit: bread and wine are changed into the Body and Blood of Christ; sweet-smelling oils become holy chrism; ordinary water is changed into holy water. Simultaneously, the transformation of those who participate in the sacrament occurs: in Baptism we are changed from the old man to the new by being born anew; in the Eucharist we are changed into members of the body of Christ by being united to Christ. In Marriage two people become "one flesh" (Gen 2.24), one body, the gap is bridged between division and unity, between being alienated and being at one with each other. This union happens thanks to the power of the mutual love of the spouses and the action of God's grace.

Jug for wine. Ancient Israel. 1st c.

Turning water into wine, moreover, is a symbol of the transformation of everyday life into a feast. The marital union, blessed by Christ, a union in which the Lord is invisibly present, is to become the unceasing feast of the spouses' ongoing revelation of the divine countenance within each other, the unending transformation of their joint daily life into one great feast.

9.3. The Sacrament of Unction (or Anointing of the Sick)

The sacrament of Anointing (or Unction) is a sacred action performed over gravely ill people. The Apostle James asks in his Epistle: "Is anyone among you sick?" And he then says that the sick person should call for the presbyters of the Church, who should "pray over him, anointing him with oil in the name of the Lord. And the prayer of faith will save the sick, and the Lord will raise him up. And if he has committed sins, he will be forgiven" (Jas 5.14–15).

Following these words, which reflect the practice of the early Church, the sacrament of Anointing involves the participation of several priests (seven, according to the Church's traditions). They come to the sick person, pray for his healing, and anoint him with consecrated oil, while passages are read from the Epistles and the Gospel.

In many parishes there is a practice of "general anointing," which is performed in church by a number of priests over those who wish to receive the sacrament (not necessarily only over those who are gravely ill).

In the sacrament of Unction, the priests ask not only for the healing of the sick person, but also for the forgiveness of his sins. There is a notion that in the sacrament of Anointing forgotten sins are forgiven and that in this manner it is a supplement to Confession. This is a misconception. Confession and Anointing are two different sacraments: the aim of the former is the healing of spiritual sicknesses (sins), while the aim of the latter is the **healing of physical infirmities**. At the same time, as one is closely linked to the other and bodily healing cannot occur without spiritual healing, the order of anointing includes prayers not only for the return of bodily health, but also for the forgiveness of sins.

The view of Unction as a ritual preparation for death, which was common in the past, should also be regarded as mistaken. The sacrament can be performed over someone who is close to death in the hope that God will accomplish a miracle and return him to life. But it is not a *viaticum*[2] in the way that Confession and Communion are for a dying Christian.

[2] Latin word meaning "provision for a journey."

---

[i] Philaret of Moscow, *Catechism* 361, p. 501.

9.4. Holy Orders

In the sacrament of Holy Orders, there are three sacred actions performed only by bishops: ordinations to the offices of deacon, priest, and bishop. The first two are performed by one bishop, but the third by an assembly of bishops (no fewer than two or three). All of these sacred actions occur during the Divine Liturgy and are celebrated with a marked solemnity. Special prayers are offered, which state that the divine grace, which always heals what is infirm and completes what is wanting, sets apart a particular person for a particular ministry.

The Church believes that it is **God Himself who selects a person for holy ministry** and that it is His grace that is poured out through the laying on of hands by one or several bishops.

Only a man with the appropriate qualities and theological education and with no canonical impediments to ordination can become a cleric of the Orthodox Church.[1] A deacon or priest may be married, but he must be married before ordination. Bishops are chosen from the ranks of the celibate clergy.[2]

9.5. Church Rites

There is a whole series of sacred actions that are counted as church rites. The difference between a sacrament and a rite is not essential to the Christian faith: this difference is conditional and it appeared rather late in the Church's history. The entire life of the Church bears a sacramental character and many sacred actions that do not belong to the category of sacraments have the characteristic features of the sacraments.

[1] One such impediment, for example, would be the second marriage of the candidate or of his wife.

[2] In the Orthodox Church all bishops are monks.

Priest's Liturgical Vestments

Priests of the Orthodox Church wear special clothes during services. They remind us of the garments of Christ and point to the grace of God given to priests, the height and dignity of their church service.

1. Phelonion

(Greek, to shine)

Sleeveless outer liturgical garment. It is symbolic of the robe that was put on Christ by the soldiers.

2. Epitrachelion (stole)

(Greek, around the neck)

Long wide stole worn around the neck with two ends sown together as it comes down on the front. No liturgical functions can be served without the priest's wearing the epitrachelion.

3. Palitsa

An award. A diamond shaped piece of cloth that hangs over a shoulder by one of the corners over the right hip. It is a symbolic sword that represents the Gospel as the "sword of the Spirit" (Eph 6.17).

4. Sticharion

Long bright garment. Symbolizes the tunic of the Savior. Derived from the liturgical clothing of the Old Testament high priests. The lower liturgical vestment of a priest. Worn during the Liturgy.

5. Kamilavka

Church award. Colors: red, purple, and black. Derived from a camel hair cap worn in the Middle East. Symbolizes Christ's crown of thorns.

8. Cuffs

Narrow cuffs, fastened with laces. They symbolize the fetters on the hands of Christ.

9. Nabedrennik

The first award for a priest for diligent service. A rectangular piece of cloth, worn on a ribbon at the left hip. Symbolizes the Four Gospels, i.e., the word of God, with which the priest must be armed as a spiritual sword.

6. Pectoral Cross

The main symbol of the priest is a minister in the image of Christ Himself. The prototype of the pectoral cross is a box with relics in the shape of a cross, which believers wore on their chests in the first centuries. In some Orthodox Churches all priests wear a pectoral cross. In other Churches only distinguished priests can wear it.

7. Belt

Worn over the cassock and stole. Symbolizes the towel that Christ wore when washing the disciples' feet at the Last Supper.

Colors of vestments on feast days

The color of the priest's vestments depends on the holiday that falls on the day of the service.

- **Gold** (yellow)—worn throughout the year except when other colors are worn (see below)
- **Red**—feast days of martyrs
- **Blue**—feast days of the Theotokos
- **Green**—Palm Sunday, Pentecost, Day of the Holy Spirit, feast days of monastic saints
- **White**—Pascha, Nativity of Christ, Epiphany, Ascension and Transfiguration of the Lord, memorial Saturdays, days of remembrance of angels
- **Purple**—Sundays and Saturdays of Great Lent, holidays in honor of the Cross of the Lord
- **Black**—weekdays of Lent

Thus, for example, tonsuring for the monastic life is a rite that in structure and content is reminiscent of the rite of Baptism. Monks and nuns are those people who have renounced the world and who have given vows of chastity, poverty, and obedience to the Church, who are called to prayer and an ascetic way of life. Embarking upon the monastic life is done through a rite in which the person receives a new name, worldly clothes are removed, and he or she is vested with monastic robes, all former sins are forgiven, and the new monk or nun becomes a member of the monastic community.

The rite of the blessing of the waters, which is celebrated on the feast of the Lord's Baptism, bears many similarities to the Eucharist. The priest and the community pray, and the Holy Spirit comes down upon the water, changing it into a great holy object that the faithful drink with reverence for the purification and sanctification of their souls and bodies, and they sprinkle their homes with it.

Rites linked to dying and death have great meaning. **The Church treats the dying with special attention** by surrounding them with her love. It is very important to invite a priest to come to a dying person while he is still conscious, so that he can make his Confession and receive Holy Communion. Relatives often postpone inviting a priest until the last minute so as not to frighten the dying person with the thought of death. This is wrong and even irreverent behavior, and because of this the dying are often deprived of the last rites.

The Church teaches us that we should not fear death and, if the person is dying but is unaware of it, the fact that he is dying should not be concealed from him. The priest can help the dying person to meet his end with dignity, fearlessly, and peacefully; he can help him cleanse his conscience through Confession and by giving him Communion before he enters eternity.

When someone has breathed his last, the priest reads special prayers over him and then (as a rule on the third day) the funeral service is held for the deceased. The body is brought into the church and loved ones are present as they say farewell. Then the body of the departed is taken to the cemetery and consigned to the earth. The priest takes part in this as well.

There are also other church rites linked to various events in a person's life, for example, the rite of blessing a house or apartment, a car or other means of transport, prayers for children for the beginning of the school year, prayer services for health, and various types of prayers for the departed. These rites and sacred actions are performed by the priest at the request of the faithful: thanks to these prayers, various aspects of human life and everyday objects become consecrated and receive the Church's blessing.

Assignment:

Read the Gospel of John. Try to answer these questions to yourself: Am I ready to receive Jesus Christ as God and Savior? Do I want to learn that love to which He has called us? Do I want to be a full-fledged member of the community of His disciples?

Read the Creed and try to learn it by heart.

Read the "Our Father" and learn it by heart.

If you have read this Catechism with the aim of deepening your knowledge of the Orthodox faith, then turn to the Afterword.

If you have not yet been baptized and wish to be baptized, or if you want to baptize your child, then speak with a priest to arrange a date for the celebration of this sacrament. Read the Afterword after the Baptism has been performed.

Afterword

To be a Christian does not mean simply to know the Creed, it does not mean simply to visit church regularly and receive Communion; it is also to **live as a Christian**. And to live as a Christian is to live not according to the standards of "this world," but by different rules and laws. It presupposes that we must be ready to go against the current; it requires spiritual heroism, and in situations of direct persecution it requires the ability to confess one's faith and die a martyr's death. Jesus was the first to tread this path, and He did not indicate any other way to His followers.

Try to **read the Gospel every day**—a chapter or a section,[1] or at least a few verses. Put the Gospel in a place where it can be seen (on the work table or bedside table) and turn to it as often as possible. When you read it, Christ will be invisibly present in your life, His living voice will resound within you and will find a response in your heart. The Gospel is the school of the religious life. Even if you have read a particular narrative many times and already know it almost by heart, it can be revealed to you afresh in an unexpected way.

I would like to offer you some advice founded upon the experience of many people: if you have a complete Bible, do not attempt to read it all at once in one go. Begin with the New Testament: read at first only the four Gospels, then try to read the Book of Acts and the Catholic Epistles. Before reading the Epistles of St Paul, go to the Old Testament and read the first two books from it—Genesis and Exodus. Then return to the Gospels and read them anew, and then turn to the Epistles of Paul.

Reading the Bible in this order will help you to become familiar with it, to feel its inner rhythm, to grasp the interconnection between the Old and New Testa-

[1] In modern editions the Gospel is divided into chapters, while in liturgical editions it is divided into "pericopes," smaller sections addressing a single topic.

ments. You can then journey independently through the Bible, choosing those books that you find interesting.

Try to **read the Psalter every day**—at least one or two psalms.[2] This biblical book contains very different prayers, ranging from those expressing affliction to those expressing joy, prayers both long and short. The entire spectrum of the experience of prayer is reflected in the Psalter, and no matter what spiritual, emotional, or physical state we may be in, we can always find in the Psalter something suitable for us.

Begin each day with prayer and end each day with prayer. To do so, make use of an *Orthodox Prayer Book*. It contains morning and evening prayers, the special prayers that are read before and after Holy Communion, as well as other prayers for various moments in life. But do not limit yourself to the prayers in the book: do not forget to pray in your own words also. After personal prayer, family prayer is important: it strengthens the family as a single whole and helps its members to feel part of the "domestic church."

If you are married, but your other half has not yet come to the faith and the Church, remember that "the unbelieving husband is sanctified by the wife, and the unbelieving wife is sanctified by the husband" (1 Cor 7.14). Never try to force your loved ones to believe in God, never drag them to church, never try to convince them through exhortations and reproaches. Simply live the life of a Christian, accomplish good, go to church, share with your loved ones the grace that has been communicated to you. They will come to the faith and the Church by themselves when they see the beneficial effect your faith exercises upon you.

Share everything that you have learned with your children. Do not be afraid if they do not understand

[2] In the Orthodox Church the Psalter is divided into twenty parts, each called a *kathisma*, from the Greek meaning "to sit," since the faithful usually sit when the psalms are being read in church. Many Christians will read one *kathisma* per day.

everything or are puzzled when they come into contact with the faith and the Church. There can be nothing but benefit for them by participating in church life. They will thank you for the rest of their lives for having brought them up in the faith and having given to them that which is most important of all—that is, God.

Try to **attend church services no less than once a week**, and do not neglect the great church feasts. Study the divine services, try to grasp their meaning without getting frustrated when the language is difficult to understand. Let the church become a spiritual home for you and for your children.

Try to **go to Confession regularly and receive Holy Communion regularly.** Cleanse your soul and heart from the evil that has accumulated there, do not be afraid to open up your soul before God and the priest. With the fear of God and faith approach the chalice of Holy Communion when receiving God within yourself. Guard the holiness of the Body and Blood of Christ: do not allow earthly cares and worries to engulf that special, reverential feeling of God's closeness that comes from Holy Communion.

Observe the fasts that have been instituted by the Church insofar as your strength allows. The Church established them not in order to torment you, but for your physical and spiritual health. But remember that the observance of the fasts is not a goal in itself, nor is better health. The most important thing is spiritual health—it cannot be exchanged for anything, and nothing can substitute for it. All of church life is aimed at this, including the fasts.

Church life is not to be a burden, but a joy. Again and again recall the words of the Apostle Paul: "**Rejoice always. Pray without ceasing. In everything give thanks**" (1 Thess 5.16–18). Let these words become your motto. Do not seek joy in things where it does not exist: in entertainments, money, vices, and love of the passions. Seek it where it truly is: in God, the fount of all

Christ Patocrator. Mosaic cathedral Hagia Sofia. Byzantium. 12th c.

joy and happiness. Earthly joys come and go quickly, but joy in God is something that no one can take from you (cf. Jn 16.22).

Life within the Church does not remove us from problems and sorrows, but it gives us the strength to endure sorrows with tranquility and joy, to solve the problems that arise with confidence. Life in the Church will not make us any more prosperous than other people, but it imparts meaning and content to our lives, including those sufferings that inevitably befall us. These sufferings and trials will not break us, for the steadfast support of faith will always protect us from falling into despair and despondency.

The Church always comes to our aid in difficult moments. The Church helps us to endure sickness patiently when it visits us; she comforts us when we grieve for a loved one who has departed for the other world, and helps us to maintain a living connection with him through prayer and commemoration of the dead; she blesses all good undertakings; she fortifies us in accomplishing good; and she teaches us to recognize danger and temptations by distinguishing between good and evil.

The Church can transform all of your life into a feast if you so desire. Do not abandon God. **Live in Christ**: sustain your soul and body with His Body and Blood, take from Him the power of grace, learn from Him wisdom, patience, humility, meekness, and kindness. Hurry to do good, fight evil. Be a Christian not in words, but in deeds.

And the Lord will be with you always!

Photography:

Inokinia Ksenia Belova – 245
Fr Seraphim Chang – 121
Vladimir Eshtokin – 48, 95, 100, 143, 175 (photo of the mosaic), 197, 201, 206, 267 (photo of the mosaic)
Natalia Fedorova – 168
Dn Maksim Gerb – 189
Eduard Gordeev – 171
Aleksander Igonin – 239
Alexey Izmailov – 156
Denis Makhanko – 104
Yulia Makoveychuk – 71, 109, 249
Vladimir Orlov– 161
Patriarch of Moscow and all Rus' Communications Department – 144, 241
Andrew Prather – 192, 194, 233, 243
Archpriest Andrey Rassanov – 208
Andrey Rybakov – 268
Saint Petersburg Theological Academy – 191, 234
Olesya Sazanova – 101
Michael Sellas Photography – 229
Elena Sysoeva – 18
Polina Teis – 235
Nadezhda Tkachenko – 103, 107, 111, 253
Sergey Voronin – 184
Dn Alexander Woodill – 93
Valeriy Zaharov – 214
Mikhail Zykov – 96
Photo of the Iconostasis (202–203) provided by furniture company Nikolaeff.su

The Holy Mountain (Mount Athos)

Hilarion Alfeyev

Jesus Christ: His Life & Teaching Series

Volume 1: *The Beginning of the Gospel*

In this first volume, Metropolitan Hilarion sets the stage for a deeper understanding of Christ and His Gospel. An overview of biblical scholarship helps readers to understand the various quests for the "historical Jesus" and to place such questions in the proper context. The Orthodox Church sees in Jesus Christ both the historical Jesus of Nazareth and God the Word made flesh. Drawing on biblical scholarship and the writings of the Church Fathers, Metropolitan Hilarion then explores Christ's birth and childhood, "The Beginning of the Gospel."

Paperback • 6×9 • 578 pp. • 978-0-88141-608-4

Volume 2: *The Sermon on the Mount*

This volume focuses entirely on the Sermon on the Mount, examining the Beatitudes, the Lord's Prayer, and other teachings of the Lord in light of both current scholarship and the Church's perennial tradition.

Paperback • 6×9 • 444 pp. • 978-0-88141-653-4

Volume 3: *The Miracles of Jesus*

Metropolitan Hilarion Alfeyev examines Jesus' miracles in their scriptural and historical context, helping us to understand their deeper meaning and to see how they reveal the true identity of Jesus Christ—our Lord and God and Savior.

Paperback • 6x9 • 456 pp. • 978-0-88141-669-5

Volume 4: *The Parables of Jesus*

JESUS CHRIST | HIS LIFE & TEACHING | VOLUME 4

The Parables of Jesus

METROPOLITAN HILARION ALFEYEV

In this volume, Metropolitan Hilarion explores the most distinct aspect of Jesus' teaching ministry: His parables. The parables are explored from multiple angles, giving due consideration both to modern biblical scholarship and the insights it can give, as well as the ancient tradition of the Church and the extensive commentaries of the Church Fathers.

Paperback • 6×9 • 428 pp. • 978-0-88141-698-5

Volume 5: *The Lamb of God*

JESUS CHRIST | HIS LIFE & TEACHING | VOLUME 5

The Lamb of God

METROPOLITAN HILARION ALFEYEV

The Fourth Gospel is remarkably unique and beautiful, and in this book, Metropolitan Hilarion guides readers to a deeper understanding of St John's unique perspective. As in all the books in this series, the text engages with the ancient tradition of the Church as well as the findings and theories of modern scholars, helping to weigh and analyze everything from an Orthodox perspective, as the author brings out of his treasure things new and old (Mt 13.52).

Paperback • 6×9 • 978-0-88141-747-0

Coming Soon: Volume 6: *Death and Resurrection*

As the sixth and final book in the series of studies on the life and teaching of Jesus Christ, Metropolitan Hilarion's book *Death and Resurrection* is entirely devoted to the events that unfolded over several days and marked the end of the earthly history of Jesus Christ — the Son of God and the Son of Man.

What do the evangelists tell us about the last days, hours, and minutes of His life? How do they describe His Resurrection? Why do their accounts of these events vary so greatly and how reliable are they? Why did Jesus' life end in such a painful and ignominious death? What is the significance of Jesus' death for Christians, and why does the Resurrection of Christ remain the main feast of the Christian Church, the centerpiece of Christian theology? Why does the story of the last days of Christ's earthly life continue twenty centuries later to have such a powerful spiritual and emotional impact on millions of people? These and many other are the questions this book seeks to answer.

We hope this book has been enjoyable and edifying for your spiritual journey toward our Lord and Savior Jesus Christ.

One hundred percent of the net proceeds of all SVS Press sales directly support the mission of St Vladimir's Orthodox Theological Seminary to train priests, lay leaders, and scholars to be active apologists of the Orthodox Christian Faith. However, the proceeds only partially cover the operational costs of St Vladimir's Seminary. To meet our annual budget, we rely on the generosity of donors who are passionate about providing theological education and spiritual formation to the next generation of ordained and lay servant leaders in the Orthodox Church.

Donations are tax-deductible and can be made at www.svots.edu/donate. We greatly appreciate your generosity.

To engage more with St Vladimir's Orthodox Theological Seminary, please visit:

www.svots.edu
online.svots.edu
www.svspress.com
www.instituteofsacredarts.com

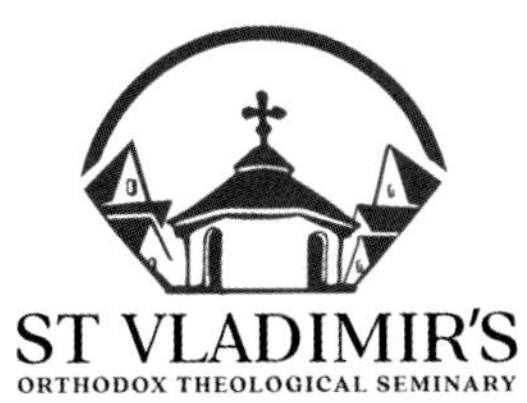

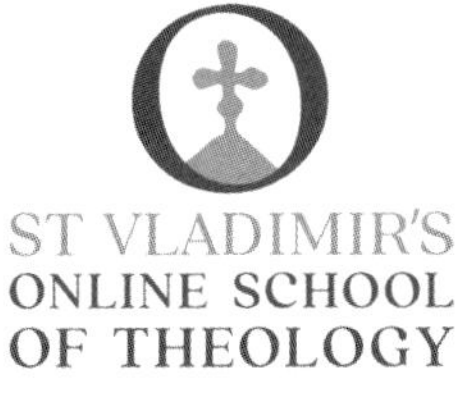